Physical Science Experiments

EXPERIMENTS FOR FUTURE SCIENTISTS

Physical Science Experiments

Edited by Aviva Ebner, Ph.D.

CHELSEA HOUSE
An Infobase Learning Company

PHYSICAL SCIENCE EXPERIMENTS

Chelsea House
An imprint of Infobase Learning
132 West 31st Street
New York NY 10001

Library of Congress Cataloging-in-Publication Data
Physical science experiments/edited by Aviva Ebner.
    p.cm.—(Experiments for future scientists)
Includes bibliographical references and index.
ISBN 978-1-60413-855-9
1. Physical sciences—Experiments—Juvenile literature. I. Ebner, Aviva. II. Title. III. Series.
Q164.P723 2011
507.8—dc22
                            2010048214

Chelsea House books are available at special discounts when purchased in bulk quantities for businesses, associations, institutions, or sales promotions. Please call our Special Sales Department in New York at (212) 967-8800 or (800) 322-8755.

You can find Chelsea House on the World Wide Web at http://www.infobasepublishing.com

Editor: Frank K. Darmstadt
Copy Editor for A Good Thing, Inc.: Milton Horowitz
Project Coordination: Aaron Richman
Art Director: Howard Petlack
Production: Shoshana Feinstein
Illustrations: Hadel Studios
Cover printed by: Yurchak Printing, Landisville, Pa.
Book printed and bound by: Yurchak Printing, Landisville, Pa.
Date printed: June 2011
Printed in the United States of America

10 9 8 7 6 5 4 3 2 1

This book is printed on acid-free paper.

Contents

Preface

Educational representatives from several states have been meeting to come to an agreement about common content standards. Because of the No Child Left Behind Act, there has been a huge push in each individual state to teach to the standards. Teacher preparation programs have been focusing on lesson plans that are standards-based. Teacher evaluations hinge on evidence of such instruction, and various districts have been discussing merit pay for teachers linked to standardized test scores.

The focus in education has shifted to academic content rather than to the learner. In the race to raise test scores, some schools no longer address all areas of a well-rounded education and have cut elective programs completely. Also, with "high-stakes" standardized testing, schools must demonstrate a constant increase in student achievement to avoid the risk of being taken over by another agency or labeled by it as failing. The appreciation of different talents among students is dwindling; a one-size-fits-all mentality has taken its place. While innovative educators struggle to teach the whole child and recognize that each student has his or her own strengths, teachers are still forced to teach to the test. Perhaps increasing test scores helps close the gap between schools. However, are we creating a generation of students not prepared for the variety of careers available to them? Many students have not had a fine-arts class, let alone been exposed to different fields in science. We *must* start using appropriate strategies for helping all students learn to the best of their abilities. The first step in doing this is igniting a spark of interest in a child.

Experiments for Future Scientists is a six-volume series designed to expose students to various fields of study in grades five to eight (though many of the experiments can be easily adapted to lower elementary or high school level), which are the formative middle school years when students are eager to explore the world around them. Each volume focuses on a different scientific discipline and alludes to possible careers or fields of study related to those disciplines. Each volume contains 20 experiments with a detailed introduction, a step-by-step experiment that can be done in a classroom or at home, thought-provoking questions, and suggested Further Reading sources to stimulate the eager student. Of course, Safety Guidelines are provided, as well as Tips for Teachers who implement the lessons. A Scope and Sequence Chart and lists for Grade Level and Setting help the teacher with alignment to content standards, while the experiments themselves help students and adults think outside the paradigm of typical activities used in most science programs.

Science is best learned by "doing." Hands-on activities and experiments are essential, not only for grasping the concepts but also for generating excitement in today's youth. In a world of video games, benchmark tests, and fewer course choices, the experiments in these books will bring student interest back to learning. The goal is to open a child's eyes to the wonders of science and perhaps imbue some "fun" that will inspire him or her to pursue a future in a field of science. Perhaps this series will inspire some students to become future scientists.

— Aviva Ebner, Ph.D.
Faculty, University of Phoenix Online;
Faculty, Brandman University; and
Educational Consultant/Administrator K-12
Granada Hills, California

Acknowledgments

I thank the following people for their assistance and contributions to this book: Mindy Perris, science education expert, New York City Board of Education District 24, for her suggestions and samples of experiments; Janet Balekian, administrator/science educator of SIAtech schools in Los Angeles, for experiment suggestions; Boris Sinofsky, retired Los Angeles Unified School District science teacher and mentor, for his evaluation of experiments; Dr. Esther Sinofsky, Director of Instructional Media Services for Los Angeles Unified School District, for assisting with research; Michael Miller, educator, and Cassandra Ebner, college student, for their help with the glossary and index; Aaron Richman of A Good Thing, Inc., for his publishing services, along with Milton Horowitz, also of A Good Thing, Inc., for always providing support and a personal touch to any project; and Frank K. Darmstadt, executive editor, Chelsea House, for his consistent hard work and his confidence in me.

This volume is dedicated to the 2007–2008 staff and students of LEAP Academy, which was located in Chatsworth, California. A fine group of individuals became a cohesive community and showed that everyone has the opportunity to succeed.

Introduction

Physical science encompasses a broad range of topics. Generally, the physical sciences include the study of non-living systems—often including space and earth sciences—but are mainly focused on chemistry and physics. Study of physical science can include chemical thermodynamics, nuclear chemistry, organic chemistry, motion, gravity, energy, molecular theory, waves, electricity, magnetism, and light. Considering the broad spectrum covered by the physical sciences, it is impossible for a single volume to encompass all areas. Rather, this volume is intended to open the eyes of children to a snapshot of some of the areas of science about which they may know little, hopefully igniting a spark that promotes further study in one or more of these subjects.

By promoting children's interest in a field of science, it is hoped that children will follow their curiosity to further explore in a specific area. A recent article in the *San Francisco Chronicle,* dated July 25, 2010, discussed that students are more motivated and engaged in school when they understand the ramifications of subjects in terms of careers later in life. Traditionally, students learn chemistry or physics. However, by engaging students in the intricacies of specialized areas within these fields, we are more likely to spur them on for additional study and make connections to possible future career choices.

Physical Science Experiments is one volume of a six-volume set called Experiments for Future Scientists that promotes interest in science and technology via high-interest, hands-on activities. Students experience the wonders of discovered wavelengths of light outside the visible light spectrum in "Testing Items With a Black Light" and "Detecting Infrared Radiation." They learn more about the behavior of light by conducting an experiment such as "Determining What Color of Light Shines Brightest Through Fog" and making three-dimensional images in "Creating a Hologram." Students can experiment with chemistry by "Making Bath Fizzers," "Testing Liquids for Use in Plaster," "Creating a Geode," "Using Chemicals to Make Soap," "Testing the Dissolution Rate of Lactase," and "Using Kitchen Chemistry to Make Glue." They can learn about energy through "Examining the Energy in a Peanut" and "Exothermic and Endothermic Reactions." Heat is studied in "Testing the Effect of Heat on

Egg Coagulation" and "Using Steam to Power a Boat." Students can learn about physics by "Creating a Magnetic Linear Accelerator" and "Throwing a Curveball."

These are just some of the experiments prepared for children in this volume. All activities are supported with background information and follow-up observation questions. The "Our Findings" section provides answers to all questions. There are "Tips for Teachers," a "Scope and Sequence Chart" to align to national standards, "Setting" suggestions for proper areas in which to conduct the experiments, "Grade Level" recommendations for each experiment, "Safety Guidelines" to ensure that proper techniques are followed, and a "Glossary" of terms. Furthermore, each experiment has a "Further Reading" section to encourage students to continue study in the area of science linked to the experiment and, at the end of the volume for even more possibilities, an "Appendix of Useful Charts and Diagrams" and an "Internet Resources" section.

Many schools and districts are already aware of the importance of encouraging study in the subject areas of physics and chemistry as early as possible. According to an October 6, 2010, article by Erik Robelen—education reporter and blogger—entitled "Computer Science Education Getting Short Shrift, Study Finds," in an issue of *Education Week*, computer science courses are being removed from high schools and replaced with courses emphasizing science, technology, engineering, and mathematics (STEM). Robelen reported for the same news source in an October 29, 2010, article entitled "Obama Plays Cheerleading Role for STEM Education" that the White House has been backing STEM initiatives, with President Obama personally hosting events that highlight the sciences for young students.

Furthermore, states competing for "Race to the Top" funds from the federal government are finding that proposals focused on STEM were given highest consideration among other proposals. This is likely due to the small numbers of students pursuing STEM education at the college level in the United States. The number of women pursuing such studies is even smaller. Since educators and parents can have a big influence in encouraging young students to pursue their interests, it has become the focus of education in the United States to make STEM classes available as early as possible in a student's educational process, then nurture this interest with the hopes of increasing the number of students entering STEM majors at United States universities.

Making STEM study accessible is not enough. Not only must students be exposed to the study of science, studies must also be presented in a manner that promotes a high level of interest. Hands-on experiments and activities are among the best ways to generate and maintain student interest in the sciences.

Scientists have changed the world for thousands of years. It is time to create the next generation of scientists. It is our hope that the experiments in this book encourage young minds to pursue their talents in the field of science.

Safety Guidelines

REVIEW BEFORE STARTING ANY EXPERIMENT

Each experiment includes special safety precautions that are relevant to that particular project. These do not include all the basic safety precautions that are necessary whenever you are working on a scientific experiment. For this reason, it is absolutely necessary that you read and remain mindful of the General Safety Precautions that follow. Experimental science can be dangerous and good laboratory procedure always includes following basic safety rules. Things can happen quickly while you are performing an experiment—for example, materials can spill, break, or even catch on fire. There will not be time after the fact to protect yourself. Always prepare for unexpected dangers by following the basic safety guidelines during the entire experiment, whether or not something seems dangerous to you at a given moment.

We have been quite sparing in prescribing safety precautions for the individual experiments. For one reason, we want you to take very seriously the safety precautions that are printed in this book. If you see it written here, you can be sure that it is here because it is absolutely critical.

Read the safety precautions here and at the beginning of each experiment before performing each lab activity. It is difficult to remember a long set of general rules. By rereading these general precautions every time you set up an experiment, you will be reminding yourself that lab safety is critically important. In addition, use your good judgment and pay close attention when performing potentially dangerous procedures. Just because the book does not say "Be careful with hot liquids" or "Don't cut yourself with a knife" does not mean that you can be careless when boiling water or using a knife to punch holes in plastic bottles. Notes in the text are special precautions to which you must pay special attention.

GENERAL SAFETY PRECAUTIONS

Accidents can be caused by carelessness, haste, or insufficient knowledge. By practicing safety procedures and being alert while conducting experiments, you can avoid taking an unnecessary risk. Be sure to check the individual experiments in this book for additional safety regulations and adult supervision requirements. If you will be working in a laboratory, do not work alone. When you are working off site, keep in groups with a minimum of three students per group, and follow school rules and state legal requirements for the number of supervisors required. Ask an adult supervisor with basic training in first aid to carry a small first-aid kit. Make sure everyone knows where this person will be during the experiment.

PREPARING

- Clear all surfaces before beginning experiments.
- Read the entire experiment before you start.
- Know the hazards of the experiments and anticipate dangers.

PROTECTING YOURSELF

- Follow the directions step by step.
- Perform only one experiment at a time.
- Locate exits, fire blanket and extinguisher, master gas and electricity shut-offs, eyewash, and first-aid kit.
- Make sure there is adequate ventilation.
- Do not participate in horseplay.
- Do not wear open-toed shoes.
- Keep floor and workspace neat, clean, and dry.
- Clean up spills immediately.
- If glassware breaks, do not clean it up by yourself; ask for teacher assistance.
- Tie back long hair.
- Never eat, drink, or smoke in the laboratory or workspace.
- Do not eat or drink any substances tested unless expressly permitted to do so by a knowledgeable adult.

USING EQUIPMENT WITH CARE

- Set up apparatus far from the edge of the desk.
- Use knives or other sharp, pointed instruments with care.

- Pull plugs, not cords, when removing electrical plugs.
- Clean glassware before and after use.
- Check glassware for scratches, cracks, and sharp edges.
- Let your teacher know about broken glassware immediately.
- Do not use reflected sunlight to illuminate your microscope.
- Do not touch metal conductors.
- Take care when working with any form of electricity.
- Use alcohol-filled thermometers, not mercury-filled thermometers.

USING CHEMICALS

- Never taste or inhale chemicals.
- Label all bottles and apparatus containing chemicals.
- Read labels carefully.
- Avoid chemical contact with skin and eyes (wear safety glasses or goggles, lab apron, and gloves).
- Do not touch chemical solutions.
- Wash hands before and after using solutions.
- Wipe up spills thoroughly.

HEATING SUBSTANCES

- Wear safety glasses or goggles, apron, and gloves when heating materials.
- Keep your face away from test tubes and beakers.
- When heating substances in a test tube, avoid pointing the top of the test tube toward other people.
- Use test tubes, beakers, and other glassware made of Pyrex™ glass.
- Never leave apparatus unattended.
- Use safety tongs and heat-resistant gloves.
- If your laboratory does not have heatproof workbenches, put your Bunsen burner on a heatproof mat before lighting it.
- Take care when lighting your Bunsen burner; light it with the airhole closed and use a Bunsen burner lighter rather than wooden matches.

- Turn off hot plates, Bunsen burners, and gas when you are done.
- Keep flammable substances away from flames and other sources of heat.
- Have a fire extinguisher on hand.

FINISHING UP

- Thoroughly clean your work area and any glassware used.
- Wash your hands.
- Be careful not to return chemicals or contaminated reagents to the wrong containers.
- Do not dispose of materials in the sink unless instructed to do so.
- Clean up all residues and put in proper containers for disposal.
- Dispose of all chemicals according to all local, state, and federal laws.

BE SAFETY CONSCIOUS AT ALL TIMES!

1. TESTING ITEMS WITH A BLACK LIGHT

Introduction

There are many everyday items in our households that *fluoresce*, or glow, under a *black light*. A black light is simply a lightbulb that emits light in the *ultraviolet* portion of the *electromagnetic spectrum*. Ultraviolet light is often referred to as UV light. Since ultraviolet *radiation* is outside the visible white-light spectrum of what humans can see with the naked eye, such lights are called *black lights*. Fluorescent objects absorb ultraviolet light, then immediately emit it. The emitted light has a longer *wavelength*, which we can observe, causing the glow that we see. Some items purposely contain fluorescent materials with minerals that fluoresce to make the product appear whiter, like whiteners in toothpaste.

In this experiment, you will test for the presence of fluorescence with the use of a black light.

Time Needed

30 minutes

What You Need

- handheld black light (can be purchased from novelty stores such as Spencer's Gifts™)
- 1 sheet white paper, unlined
- jar of petroleum jelly (e.g., Vaseline®)
- 2 large, clear-plastic cups
- small bottle of club soda

- vitamin B$_{12}$ tablet (available from health food stores or pharmacies)
- vinegar, 1 cup (237 ml)
- coffee stirrer
- hammer
- cup of laundry detergent that contains whiteners
- pen or pencil
- dark room

Safety Precautions

Please review and follow the safety guidelines at the beginning of this volume.

What You Do

1. Darken the room.
2. Shine the black light on the sheet of white paper.
3. Record your observations on the data table.
4. Open the jar of petroleum jelly.
5. Shine the black light on the petroleum jelly from the open top.
6. Record your observations on the data table.
7. Fill a plastic cup with club soda.
8. Shine the black light on the top of the club soda in the cup.
9. Record your observations on the data table.
10. Crush a vitamin B$_{12}$ tablet with the hammer.
11. Add the powder from the crushed tablet to a clean cup (Figure 1).

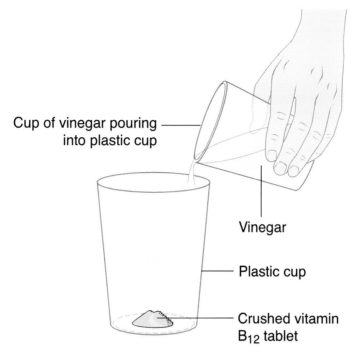

Figure 1

12. Pour 1 cup of vinegar into the cup (Figure 1).
13. Stir the contents until they are well mixed.
14. Shine the black light on the vitamin/vinegar solution.
15. Record your observations on the data table.
16. Scoop up 1 cup of whitening laundry detergent.
17. Shine the black light on the detergent.
18. Record your observations on the data table.

Data Table	
Material observed	**Observations: Did the material glow under the black light? If so, what color was the glow?**
White paper	
Petroleum jelly	

(continued)

Club soda	
Vitamin B$_{12}$ in vinegar	
Laundry detergent	

 **Observations**

1. Did all of the materials glow? If not, which ones did not glow?
2. Did the materials that glowed all glow the same color? Why or why not?
3. What causes certain items to glow in black light?

Our Findings

Please refer to the Our Findings appendix at the back of this volume.

Further Reading

"Fluorescence." *The Columbia Encyclopedia*, 6th ed. 2008. Available online. URL: http://www.encyclopedia.com/doc/1E1-fluoresc. html. Accessed June 16, 2010. Short entry explaining why certain materials emit a fluorescent glow.

Pough, Frederick. *A Field Guide to Rocks and Minerals*. Boston: Houghton Mifflin Harcourt, 1998. Includes a guide for rock and mineral identification and indicates which minerals glow with fluorescence.

Stille, Darlene. *Invisible Exposure: The Science of Ultraviolet Rays*. Mankato, MN: Compass Point Books, 2010. Illustrated book for upper-elementary and middle-school students that explains the dangers of overexposure to ultraviolet rays.

"Ultraviolet Radiation." NASA.gov. 2001. Available online. URL: http://www.nas.nasa.gov/About/Education/Ozone/radiation.html. Accessed June 16, 2010. NASA's official Web site has information about the damage caused to humans and other life on Earth from excessive exposure to certain type of ultraviolet radiation.

"Ultraviolet Rays." NASA.gov. 2007. Available online. URL: http://science.hq.nasa.gov/kids/imagers/ems/uv.html. Accessed June 16, 2010. NASA's official Web site contains information for children explaining ultraviolet light and the fact that this type of radiation is emitted by the Sun.

2. MAKING BATH FIZZERS

Introduction

There are many bath products available today to make bath time more fun. One of these is a bath fizzer, or a small dry ball which, when dropped into bath water, literally fizzes in the water. Fizzers may also color the water or add a nice *fragrance*. The science behind these fizzers is the *chemical reaction* occurring between baking soda, which is a *base*, and *citric acid*, which, as its name states, is an *acid*. This reaction produces *carbon dioxide gas*. These fizzers are made from easy-to-find chemicals. With some household chemistry, you can create your own bath fizzers and test them in your bathtub.

In this experiment, you will combine some commonly found chemicals to create your own safe-to-use bath fizzers.

Time Needed

20 minutes to prepare
2 days to complete

What You Need

- citric acid, 2 tablespoons (tbsp; 30 grams [g]) (can be purchased from a science supply company like Science Kit and Boreal Laboratories or craft stores such as Joann's or Michael's).

- cornstarch, 2 tbsp (about 30 milliliters)

- baking soda, 1/4 cup (about 58 grams)

- glass jar with lid

fragrance oil, a few drops (available at craft stores or at bath product stores such as Bath and Body Works)

 vegetable oil, 3 tbsp (about 44 ml)

 bowl

 long stirring spoon

 food coloring, any color, a few drops

 dry area

 clean, dry, empty container with a lid

 ruler

Safety Precautions

Please review and follow the safety guidelines at the beginning of this volume.

What You Do

1. Add the citric acid, cornstarch, and baking soda to the glass jar.
2. Mix the contents of the jar with the spoon (Figure 1).

Spoon for mixing contents

Glass jar

Contents: acids, cornstarch, baking soda

Figure 1

3. Add a few drops of fragrance oil.
4. Add a few drops of food coloring.

5. Tightly close the lid on the jar and shake the contents until they are thoroughly mixed.

6. Empty the contents of the jar into a bowl.

7. Slowly add the vegetable oil to the mixture while stirring constantly.

8. Shape the mixture with your hands by rolling parts of it into 1-in. to 1.5-in. balls (Figure 2).

Balled mixture, 1–1.5 in.

Figure 2

9. Allow to dry for 2 days.

10. If you will not be using the balls right away, store them in a sealed container.

11. The next time you take a bath, drop a balled mixture in the water and observe.

 **Observations**

1. What happened when you dropped the ball into the bath water?

2. Which chemicals are reacting to create this effect?

3. What chemical is being produced in this reaction?

4. What changes could you make to the ingredients to alter the scent or color of the fizzers?

Our Findings

Please refer to the Our Findings appendix at the back of this volume.

Further Reading

"Acids and Bases." *UXL Encyclopedia of Science*. 2002. Available online. URL: http://www.encyclopedia.com/doc/1G2-3438100013. html. Accessed June 14, 2010. Detailed explanation of the structure and properties of acids and bases.

"Acids and Bases Are Everywhere." Chem4kids.com. 2009. Available online. URL: http://www.chem4kids.com/files/react_acidbase.html. Accessed June 14, 2010. Explains acids and bases in simple terms for children.

Baldwin, Carol. *Acids and Bases*. Portsmouth, NH: Heinemann Library, 2004. Children's book that explains the relationships between acids and bases.

Brent, Lynnette. *Acids and Bases*. New York: Crabtree Publishing Company, 2008. Children's book for upper-elementary and middle school explaining the chemistry of acids and bases.

Oxlade, Chris. *Acids and Bases*. Portsmouth, NH: Heinemann Library, 2002. Children's book covering certain core areas of chemistry.

3. TESTING LIQUIDS FOR USE IN PLASTER

Introduction

Plaster of paris contains both *calcium carbonate* and *calcium sulfate*. Both of these chemicals are used for the production of *cement*. Plaster, like cement and most other building materials, starts off wet and then later hardens. The water used in the creation of these materials does not *evaporate*; it actually reacts with the other *substances*. Cement materials that require water are known as *hydraulic cements*. It is possible for these types of cements to harden even underwater because of the *chemical reaction* that takes place. Cements are used to bind *aggregates* together and are useful for forming strong building materials that can withstand the typical elements of the weather and environment.

In this activity, you will test different liquids to determine the liquids that produce the best consistency for plaster.

Time Needed

45 minutes

What You Need

- ✎ bag or box of plaster of paris mix
- ✎ 4 small, plastic cups
- ✎ warm water, 2 teaspoons (tsp; 10 milliliters [ml])
- ✎ water, a few teaspoons at room temperature
- ✎ salt, 1/2 tsp (2.5 ml)
- ✎ vinegar, 1 to 2 tsps (5–10 ml)

- ✎   6 plastic spoons

- ✎   wax paper, a sheet about 24 in. (61 cm) long

- ✎   masking tape

- ✎   pen

- ✎   watch, clock, or timer

Safety Precautions

Please review and follow the safety guidelines at the beginning of this volume.

What You Do

1. Using the masking tape and the pen, label each of 3 cups, respectively, water, salt water, and vinegar (Figure 1).

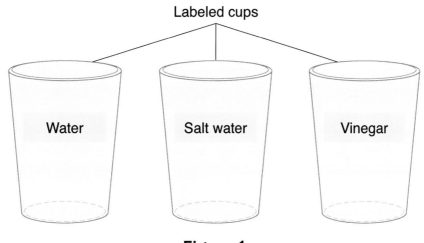

Figure 1

2. Using the masking tape and pen, label the left end of the wax paper as water, the middle as salt water, and the right side as vinegar (Figure 2).

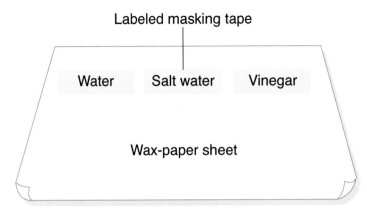

Figure 2

3. In the fourth cup, mix the salt and warm water, stirring until most of the salt is dissolved.

4. Add a heaping teaspoon of plaster mix to each of the labeled cups.

5. Add 1 tsp of water to the cup labeled "Water" and mix thoroughly. If necessary, add more water or plaster, a little bit at a time, until the mixture is a consistency thick enough to be molded.

6. Using a spoon, push the mixture out of the cup onto the area of the wax paper that is labeled "Water." If necessary, use another spoon to scrape the mixture off the first spoon.

7. Repeat steps 5 and 6 using the salt-water solution and placing the mixture on the area of the wax paper labeled "Salt water."

8. Repeat steps 5 and 6 using vinegar and placing the mixture on the area of the wax paper labeled "Vinegar."

9. After about 5 minutes, use a spoon to press down on each mound of plaster you created (Figure 3).

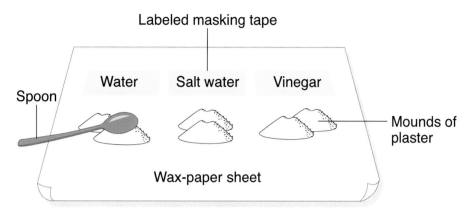

Figure 3

10. Record your observations on the data table.

11. Repeat steps 9 and 10 after another 5 minutes.

12. Repeat step 11.

Data Table			
Liquid used in mixture	**After 5 minutes**	**After 10 minutes**	**After 15 minutes**
Water			
Salt water			
Vinegar			

Observations

1. Which liquid worked the best at hardening the plaster?

2. Which liquid was the worst for hardening the plaster?

3. Why is it important that plaster or cement be hardened to the right consistency?

4. What part of this process had to do with a chemical reaction?

Our Findings

Please refer to the Our Findings appendix at the back of this volume.

Further Reading

"Cement." *The Columbia Encyclopedia*, 6th ed. 2008. Available online. URL: http://www.encyclopedia.com/doc/1E1-cement.html. Accessed June 16, 2010. Explains how cement is made and used in building.

"Concrete, Cement, and Masonry." Homedepot.com. 2010. Available online. URL: http://www.homedepot.com/Building-Materials-Concrete-Cement-Masonry/h_d1/N-5yc1vZ1xr5Zarlk/h_d2/Navigation?langId=-1&storeId=10051&catalogId=10053. Accessed June 16, 2010. Information from one of the largest home improvement stores about different building materials and how to use them.

"Gypsum." *The Columbia Encyclopedia*, 6th ed. 2008. Available online. URL: http://www.encyclopedia.com/doc/1E1-gypsum.html. Accessed June 16, 2010. Explains how gypsum is used in the formation of plaster of paris.

Hewlett, Peter. *Lea's Chemistry of Cement and Concrete*, 4th ed. Burlington, MA: Butterworth-Heinemann, 2004. Advanced text explaining the chemistry behind how cement and concrete are made and why they harden.

Plowman, John. *Plasterworks*. Cincinnati: North Light Books, 1996. Step-by-step guide to making crafts from plaster.

4. CREATING A GEODE

Introduction

Geodes are *geological* rock formations sometimes found in *volcanic* or *sedimentary* rocks. On the outside, they are simply rocks, but on the inside, they contain beautiful *crystals*. The outside of a geode is usually made of *limestone*; the crystals inside are typically *quartz*. The prevailing *theory* on geode formation is that gas bubbles form in *lava*. These spaces allow for *groundwater*, rich in *minerals*, to seep in. The *sediments* harden and form a layer of rock as the minerals *crystallize* inside. To find out what type of crystal has formed inside a geode, the geode must be cut open. Crystals might be quartz, *agate*, *gypsum*, *amethyst*, and many other types.

In this experiment, you will simulate the growth of crystals inside a geode by creating models with actual crystals.

Time Needed

30 minutes to prepare

3 days to complete

What You Need

- 6 eggs
- empty egg carton
- 2 cups (473 milliliters [ml]) boiling hot water
- 3 to 4 tablespoons (tbsp) (42.7–57 g) borax (available in the detergent section of the supermarket)

2 to 3 tbsp (28.5–42.7 g) copper sulfate (available from science supply companies such as Science Kit and Boreal Laboratories or Carolina™ Science Supply Company)

  wax paper, a piece about 1 foot long (30 cm)

  2 cups (473 ml) room temperature water

  large bowl

  2 measuring cups

  scissors

  2 stirrers

Safety Precautions

Please review and follow the safety guidelines at the beginning of this volume. Wear goggles when handling chemicals. Copper sulfate can irritate the skin and mucous membranes, so avoid eye contact and skin contact. Adult supervision is recommended when handling hot materials.

What You Do

1. Carefully crack the eggs in half, discarding the contents of the eggs (Figure 1).

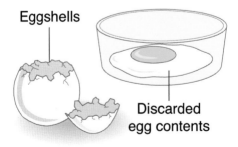

Figure 1

2. Place the squares in the egg carton spaces.

3. Cut small squares from the wax paper, just large enough to line the inside of each egg carton space (Figure 2).

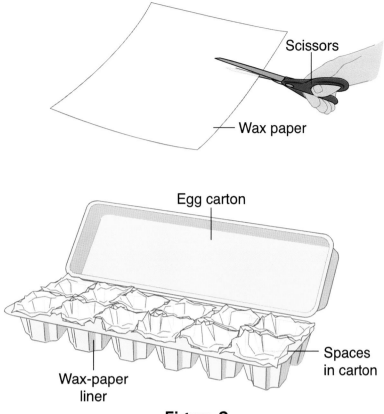

Scissors

Wax paper

Egg carton

Spaces
in carton

Wax-paper
liner

Figure 2

4. Making sure not to crack or crush the eggshells, rinse out the inside of each egg with room temperature water. You can do this over a large bowl to prevent spillage.

5. Carefully place each egg shell half on top of the wax paper in each egg carton space (Figure 3).

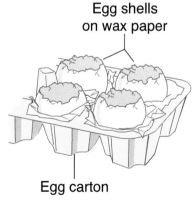

Egg shells
on wax paper

Egg carton

Figure 3

6. In one measuring cup, add borax to 1 cup (237 ml) of boiling hot water. Add the borax slowly, stirring occasionally, until the

borax is completely dissolved. Stop adding the borax when the solution is saturated, which means that it will no longer dissolve any more of the borax.

7. In the other measuring cup, repeat step 6 with the copper sulfate and 1 cup of boiling hot water.

8. Pour a small amount of the borax solution into half of the egg shells (Figure 4).

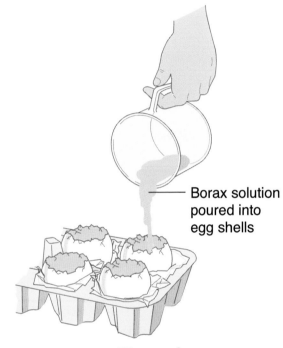

Borax solution poured into egg shells

Figure 4

9. Pour a small amount of copper sulfate solution into the rest of the egg shells.

10. Set aside the egg carton where it can remain undisturbed for at least 3 days.

11. After 3 days, observe your homemade geodes.

12. If there is solution still left in the eggshells, pour it out or allow the eggshells to dry for about a week.

 **Observations**

1. What did you observe inside the eggshells?

2. Were the crystals formed by the borax solution identical to the ones formed by the copper sulfate solution?

3. What other common solutions could you use for forming crystals?

4. How do geodes form in nature?

Our Findings

Please refer to the Our Findings appendix at the back of this volume.

Further Reading

Cross, Brad Lee. *Geodes: Nature's Treasures*. Baldwin Park, CA: Gem Guides Book Company, 2006. Explains the geode mining process and includes over 140 color photographs of geodes.

"Geode." *The Columbia Encyclopedia*, 6th ed. 2008. Available online. URL: http://www.encyclopedia.com/doc/1E1-geode.html. Accessed June 5, 2010. Short article explaining what a geode is and how it is formed.

Pabian, Roger, Brian Jackson, Peter Tandy, and John Cromartie. *Agates: Treasures of the Earth*. Ontario Canada: Firefly Books, 2006. Color photographs illustrate this book about the semi-precious-gem agate that is found inside geodes.

"Quartz." *The Columbia Encyclopedia*, 6th ed. 2008. Available online. URL: http://www.encyclopedia.com/doc/1E1-quartz.html. Accessed June 5, 2010. Information about quartz mineral crystals.

Witzke, Brian. "Geodes: A Look at Iowa's State Rock." *Iowa Department of Natural Resources Geological Survey*. 2010. Available online. URL: http://www.igsb.uiowa.edu/browse/geodes/geodes. htm. Accessed June 5, 2010. Explains not only how geodes form but also which specific crystals are typically found inside the geodes of Iowa. Includes photos.

5. THROWING A CURVEBALL

Introduction

Baseball pitchers can command large salaries if they can consistently throw pitches that strike out batters. Most good pitchers have a number of different types of pitches they can throw, including fastballs and changeups. One particularly useful pitch is the curveball, at which the batter is likely to swing and miss because the ball's *trajectory* follows a curved path. *Friction* causes the ball to spin rapidly, *clockwise* for a right-handed pitcher and *counterclockwise* for a left-handed pitcher. As the ball spins, a layer of air, called the *boundary layer*, is pulled in. Since the ball is moving forward even as it is spinning, on one side of the ball the boundary layer is moving in the same direction as the air flowing around the ball; but on the other side the boundary layer is moving in the opposite direction from the airflow. Because the two layers of air are moving in opposite directions, the airstream is slowed down, while on the other side both are moving in the same direction so the airstream moves faster. *Bernoulli's principle* states that faster moving air will exert less pressure than the slower air; as a result, this causes the ball to move either to the right or left.

In this activity, you will create a device that can throw curveballs.

Time Needed

25 minutes

What You Need

- 2 cardboard mailing tubes, 2 feet long (61 centimeters [cm]) each (cut to fit if necessary), that have a diameter larger than a Ping-Pong™ ball

- Ping-Pong™ ball

- medium sandpaper, 1 standard-sized sheet

- white glue

- black permanent marker

- ruler

- sharp scissors or knife, for cutting the mailing tube

Safety Precautions

Please review and follow the safety guidelines at the beginning of this volume. Always exercise caution when handling sharp objects. Adult supervision is recommended when handling sharp objects and tools like scissors or knives.

What You Do

1. Spread glue over the back of the sandpaper.

2. Roll the sandpaper so that the glue is on the outside (Figure 1).

Glue on back of sandpaper

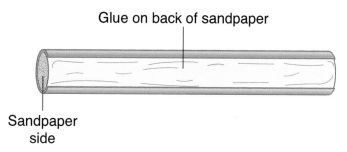

Sandpaper side

Figure 1

3. Slide the rolled sandpaper into the mailing tube on one end so that the edge of the sandpaper and the edge of the mailing tube are aligned (Figure 2).

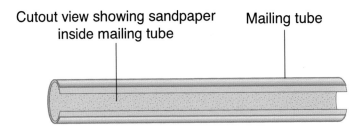

Figure 2

4. Draw a circle all around the Ping-Pong™ ball (Figure 3).

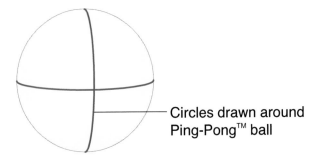

Figure 3

5. Repeat step 4 at a right angle to the first circle (Figure 3).
6. Hold the tube at the end that does not have the sandpaper, tilting it just slightly upward.
7. Insert the Ping-Pong™ ball into the tube at the sandpaper end.
8. Hold the tube horizontally and keeping it level, swing the tube through the air (Figure 4).

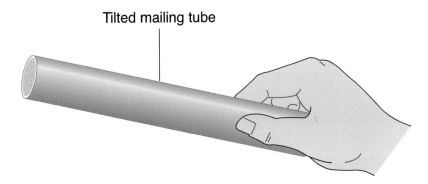

Figure 4

9. Observe the trajectory of the ball.

10. Repeat steps 6 to 9 with the mailing tube that has no sandpaper.

Observations

1. Did you notice a difference between the trajectory of the ball when you used the tube with sandpaper versus the one without it?
2. Describe the trajectory of the ball that was thrown with the tube that contained sandpaper.
3. How does this relate to Bernoulli's principle?
4. What is a practical application of this phenomenon?

Our Findings

Please refer to the Our Findings appendix at the back of this volume.

Further Reading

"Bernoulli's Principle." *The Columbia Encyclopedia*, 6th ed. 2008. Available online. URL: http://www.encyclopedia.com/doc/1E1-Bernoull.html. Accessed June 18, 2010. Short entry defining Bernoulli's Principle.

———. Aeronautics Learning Laboratory. 2009. Available online. URL: http://www.allstar.fiu.edu/aero/pic3-2.htm. Accessed June 18, 2010. Explains Bernoulli's Principle and how this explains why airplanes can fly.

———. Scienceclarified.com. 2010. Available online. URL: http://www.scienceclarified.com/everyday/Real-Life-Chemistry-Vol-3-Physics-Vol-1/Bernoulli-s-Principle.html. Accessed June 18, 2010. Explains Bernoulli's principle related to differences in air speed and pressure.

House, Tom, Gary Heil, and Steve Johnson. *The Art and Science of Pitching*. Monterey, CA: Coaches Choice Books, 2006. Featuring numerous photographs, this book details how to throw specific types of baseball pitches.

Kempf, Cheri. *The Softball Pitching Edge*. Champaign, IL: Human Kinetics, 2002. Step-by-step instruction on how to throw softball pitches. Includes photographs.

6. DIFFUSION OF MOLECULES THROUGH A BALLOON

Introduction

Everything around us consists of *matter*. Even *gases* that we cannot see are made up of *molecules*. You can observe this phenomenon by simply opening a bottle of perfume. If left open, the perfume molecules start to spread outside of the container, and you can smell the perfume, even if your nose is not directly over the bottle. Particles tend to move from an area of higher *concentration* to an area of lower concentration in a process called *diffusion*. This process occurs because the molecules create a balance known as *equilibrium*. Sometimes, the particles have to pass through a *membrane* or a *barrier* for diffusion to take place. Items that we may perceive as solid objects might actually have microscopic holes through which molecules can pass, allowing diffusion to take place.

In this experiment, you will test several items for the ability of some of their molecules to diffuse through a balloon.

Time Needed

40 minutes

What You Need

- 5 round balloons
- 5 plastic cups
- 5 medicine droppers
- vanilla extract, about 2 teaspoons (tsp; 10 ml)
- milk, about 2 tsp (10 ml)

✏   lemon juice, about 2 tsp (10 ml)

✏   vinegar, about 2 tsp (10 ml)

✏   coffee drink, about 2 tsp (10 ml)

✏   timer or clock

✏   masking tape, 5 pieces

✏   pen or marker

 ## Safety Precautions

Please review and follow the safety guidelines at the beginning of this volume.

What You Do

1. Label each of 5 cups, respectively, vanilla, milk, lemon juice, vinegar, and coffee.

2. Fill a medicine dropper with vanilla extract.

3. Squirt the contents into a balloon (Figure 1).

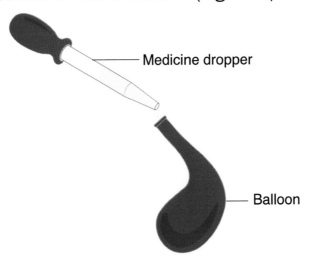

Figure 1

4. Repeat steps 2 and 3.

5. Blow up the balloon as much as you can without inhaling the contents and without popping it, while still being able to tie it closed.

6. Tie the end of the balloon securely.

7. Set the balloon, tied end down, onto the plastic cup labeled "Vanilla" (Figure 2).

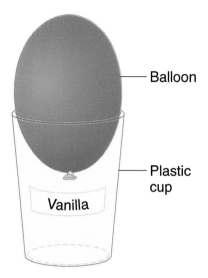

Figure 2

8. Using a fresh dropper for each different substance, repeat steps 2 to 7 with the milk, lemon juice, vinegar, and coffee, placing each substance in the appropriately labeled cup.

9. After 10 minutes, remove the balloons and smell the inside of the cups.

10. Record your observations on the data table.

Data Table	
Substance	**Odor?**
Vanilla	
Milk	
Lemon juice	
Vinegar	
Coffee	

 **Observations**

1. Which substances could you smell in the cups?

2. How do you know that some of the molecules from those substances diffused into the cup?

3. How do you know diffusion took place?

4. How could molecules travel through a solid like a balloon?

Our Findings

Please refer to the Our Findings appendix at the back of this volume.

Further Reading

Aftel, Mandy. *Essence and Alchemy*. New York: Bloomsbury Publishing, 2002. Includes everything from the history of perfumes, to humorous stories, to formulas for perfumes, to uses for perfumes.

"Diffusion." *The Columbia Encyclopedia*, 6th ed. 2008. Available online. URL: http://www.encyclopedia.com/doc/1E1-diffusio.html. Accessed June 18, 2010. Encyclopedia entry explaining the process of diffusion and concentration gradients.

"Diffusion and Osmosis." Biologycorner.com. 2010. Available online. URL: http://www.biologycorner.com/bio1/diffusion.html. Accessed June 18, 2010. Defines both terms and differentiates between diffusion and osmosis.

"Perfume." *The Columbia Encyclopedia*, 6th ed. 2008. Available online. URL: http://www.encyclopedia.com/doc/1E1-perfume. html. Accessed June 18, 2010. A brief history of perfumes and the materials used to create scents.

Turin, Luca. *The Secret of Scent*. New York: Harper Perennial, 2007. Provides the background on the development of perfumes and the science behind them.

7. TESTING THE DISSOLUTION RATE OF LACTASE

Introduction

Digestion is a *complex* process that occurs in your body to break down food to a form in which your body can use it. There are numerous *chemical reactions* that occur in your *digestive system* that allow digestion to occur at body temperature. *Enzymes* play a large role in these reactions; they are molecules that speed up these chemical reactions. One such enzyme is *lactase*, an enzyme that is typically added to the process in your small intestine. Lactase helps break down *lactose*, a component of dairy products that is a type of sugar. However, some people lack this enzyme, causing difficulty in digestion of milk products and physical *discomfort* after eating such products. This condition is known as *lactose intolerance*. Fortunately, there are over-the-counter aids available to provide this enzyme after *ingestion* of a simple tablet. There are several different brands, and though they all offer relief from the discomfort, the consumer may not be aware that some *dissolve* faster, providing quick relief.

In this experiment, you will use physical science to compare the *dissolution rates* of several brands of lactase pills to determine which one dissolves the fastest.

Time Needed

60 to 90 minutes

What You Need

✎   water, about 3 quarts (3 liters)

- ✎   microwave

- ✎   thermometer

- ✎   9 disposable plastic or wooden coffee stirrers

- ✎   stopwatch or clock with a seconds hand

- ✎   3 different brands of lactase pills, 3 pills from each brand (e.g., Lactaid,® Kirkland,® Major,® Nature's Way,® Dairy-Ease,® available at your local pharmacy)

- ✎   graduated cylinder that holds at least 8.5 ounces (oz; 250 ml)

- ✎   9 microwave beakers or clear-plastic cups that can hold at least 8.5 oz (250 ml)

Safety Precautions

Please review and follow the safety guidelines at the beginning of this volume.

What You Do

1. Measure 250 ml of water with the graduated cylinder and add it to a beaker.

2. Place the beaker of water in the microwave and heat it until the water temperature is 98.6°F (37°C). You may need to microwave the water for short periods of time, pause, measure the temperature with a thermometer, then continue heating if it is not warm enough.

3. Remove the beaker from the microwave.

4. Drop 1 pill from one of the brands of lactase into the beaker and start the stopwatch (Figure 1).

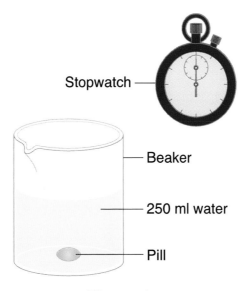

Stopwatch

Beaker

250 ml water

Pill

Figure 1

5. Stir the liquid continuously until the pill fully dissolves (Figure 2).

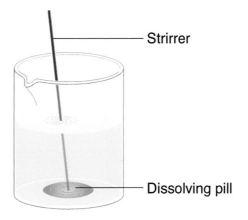

Strirrer

Dissolving pill

Figure 2

6. Record on the data table the time from the stopwatch at which the pill was completely dissolved.

7. Repeat steps 1 to 6 two more times using the same brand of pill.

8. Calculate the average time of dissolution of that brand by adding the 3 stopwatch times from the data table and dividing by 3.

9. Repeat steps 1 to 8 for the other 2 brands.

Data Table			
Trial	Time to dissolve brand 1	Time to dissolve brand 2	Time to dissolve brand 3
1			
2			
3			
Average time			

 **Observations**

1. Why was the experiment conducted using water at 98.6°F?
2. Which brand dissolved the fastest?
3. How do you think a faster dissolution rate would help someone digesting lactase?
4. Do you think all of the brands would provide equally fast relief to the user? Why or why not?
5. Which brand would you recommend to someone who needed to take lactase? Why?

Our Findings

Please refer to the Our Findings appendix at the back of this volume.

Further Reading

Aranda-Michel, Jaime, and Donald Vaughan. *Living Well With Lactose Intolerance*. New York: Avon, 1999. Explains what lactose intolerance is, what the symptoms are, and how it is treated.

Bohager, Tom. *Enzymes; What the Experts Know*. Chino Valley, AZ: One World Press, 2006. Explains the role enzymes play in digestion and other health-related issues, as well as how enzyme therapy can benefit people with specific health concerns.

"Enzyme." *The Columbia Encyclopedia*, 6th ed. 2008. Available online. URL: http://www.encyclopedia.com/doc/1E1-enzyme.html. Accessed June 6, 2010. Detailed article describing the role enzymes play in chemical reactions.

"Lactose." *The Columbia Encyclopedia*, 6th ed. 2008. Available online. URL: http://www.encyclopedia.com/doc/1E1-lactose. html. Accessed June 6, 2010. Short entry defining lactose and its sources.

Sims, Judith, and Lisette Hilton. "Lactose Intolerance." *Gale Encyclopedia of Children's Health: Infancy through Adolescence*. 2006. Available online. URL: http://www.encyclopedia.com/ doc/1G2-3447200333.html. Accessed June 6, 2010. Highly detailed article explaining the causes of lactose intolerance, its symptoms, and its treatment.

8. EXOTHERMIC AND ENDOTHERMIC REACTIONS

Introduction

Chemical reactions are often accompanied by a change in temperature. The temperature could increase or decrease depending on the type of reaction that occurs. If more energy is required to cause the reaction—for example, to break apart the *bonds* between *atoms*—than is released, then the reaction is considered *endothermic*, and the temperature goes down. If less energy was required for the reaction to occur than is released, the reaction is called *exothermic*, and the temperature goes up.

In this experiment, you will combine chemicals to produce an exothermic reaction and an endothermic reaction.

Time Needed

35 minutes

What You Need

- 3% hydrogen peroxide, 2 tablespoons (tbsp; 30 ml)
- yeast, 3 teaspoons (tsp; 15 ml)
- 2 plastic cups
- 2 thermometers
- stopwatch or watch
- partner
- vinegar, 2 tbsp (30 ml)
- baking soda, 1 tsp (5 ml)

Safety Precautions

Please review and follow the safety guidelines at the beginning of this volume.

What You Do

1. Pour the hydrogen peroxide into a cup.

2. Place the thermometer into the plastic cup and take the temperature of the hydrogen peroxide.

3. Record the temperature (Temp) on Data Table 1 under time 0.

4. Add the yeast.

5. Gently stir the yeast and hydrogen peroxide with a thermometer while checking the temperature on the thermometer and calling out the temperature readings to your partner. Your partner should record the temperatures every 10 seconds on Data Table 1.

6. Continue to do step 5 until you have reached 120 seconds.

7. Use the information from Data Table 1 to fill in the graph in Figure 1.

8. Pour 2 tbsp of vinegar into the second cup.

9. Place the second thermometer into the cup and take the temperature of the vinegar.

10. Record the temperature on Data Table 2 under time 0.

11. Add 1 tsp of baking soda to the vinegar.

12. Gently stir the baking soda and vinegar with the thermometer while checking the temperature on the thermometer and calling out the temperature (Temp) readings to your partner. He or she should record the temperatures every 3 seconds on Data Table 2.

13. Continue to do step 12 until you have reached 30 seconds.

14. Use the information from Data Table 2 to complete the graph in Figure 2.

Data Table 1												
Time (sec)	0	10	20	30	40	50	60	70	80	90	100	100	120
Temp													

Data Table 2											
Time (sec)	0	3	6	9	12	15	18	21	24	27	30
Temp											

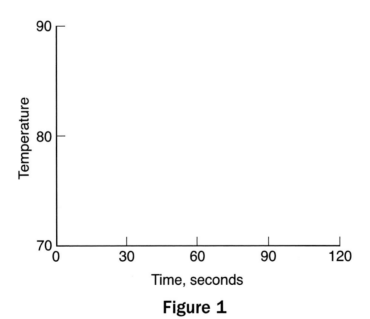

Figure 1

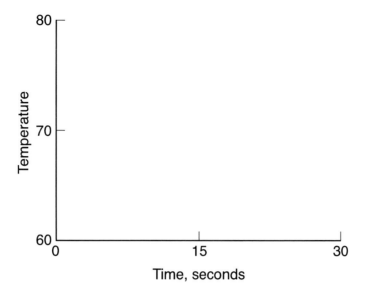

Figure 2

 **Observations**

1. Which reaction was exothermic? How do you know?
2. Which reaction was endothermic? How do you know?
3. Which reaction released energy?
4. Which reaction absorbed energy?

Our Findings

Please refer to the Our Findings appendix at the back of this volume.

Further Reading

Baldwin, Carol. *Chemical Reactions*. Mankato, MN: Heinemann, 2004. Explains the science behind chemical reactions and provides many color photographs to illustrate the information.

Carpi, Anthony. "Chemical Reactions." 2003. Available online. URL: http://www.visionlearning.com/library/module_viewer.php?mid=54. Accessed June 16, 2010. Explains the processes that occur during chemical reactions.

"Exothermic Reactions." Ewort.org.uk. 2010. Available online. URL: http://www.ewart.org.uk/science/patterns/pat9.htm. Accessed June 16, 2010. Interactive Web site that allows students to fill in the blanks concerning information about exothermic reactions.

Lew, Kristi. *Chemical Reactions*. New York: Chelsea House Publishers, 2008. Book geared toward upper-elementary and middle school students explaining chemical reactions, including endothermic and exothermic reactions.

Senese, Fred. "What Are Some Examples of Exothermic and Endothermic Processes?" 2010. Available online. URL: http://antoine.frostburg.edu/chem/senese/101/thermo/faq/exothermic-endothermic-examples.shtml. Accessed June 16, 2010. Includes a chart with specific concrete examples of exothermic and endothermic reactions.

9. EXAMINING THE ENERGY IN A PEANUT

Introduction

Energy is usually categorized in two main forms: *potential* and *kinetic*. Potential energy is stored energy that can encompass *chemical energy* stored in the *bonds* of *atoms* and *molecules*, *mechanical energy* stored in objects by tension, *nuclear energy* stored in the *nucleus* of an atom, *gravitational energy* stored in an object's height, and *electrical energy* such as that stored in a battery. Kinetic energy is the energy of motion and includes *radiant energy* that travels in *transverse waves*, *thermal energy* in the form of heat, motion energy found in moving objects, and sound that moves through *longitudinal waves*. Food has stored energy that is released by our bodies. We can demonstrate the energy stored in a food by releasing its thermal energy.

In this experiment, you will release the stored energy in a peanut and observe this release in the form of thermal energy.

Time Needed

60 minutes

What You Need

- cork
- sewing needle
- small bag or can of unsalted, shelled peanuts
- empty coffee can
- empty soup or vegetable can, smaller than the coffee can

- can opener
- hammer
- long nail
- metal skewer, such as used for barbecuing
- water, about 1 cup (about 237 ml)
- measuring cup
- thermometer
- lighter
- timer or clock
- non-flammable surface
- paper, 1 sheet, lined
- pen or pencil

Safety Precautions

Please review and follow the safety guidelines at the beginning of this volume. Adult supervision is recommended when using an open flame and handling sharp objects.

What You Do

1. Push the sharp end of the needle into an unsalted, shelled peanut (Figure 1). Do not push too hard or the peanut will break apart.

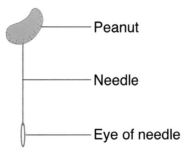

Figure 1

2. Push the opposite end of the needle (the "eye") into the center of the cork (Figure 2).

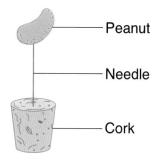

Peanut

Needle

Cork

Figure 2

3. Remove all labels from the larger coffee can.

4. Using the can opener, completely remove both the top and bottom of the can, making sure not to cut yourself on the sharp edges.

5. Hammer the nail into the side of the coffee can about 1/4 to 1/2 in. (0.64 to 1.28 centimeters [cm]) above the bottom of the can, punching a hole through the metal (Figure 3).

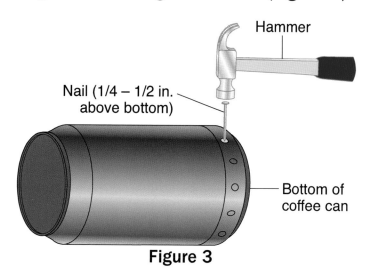

Hammer

Nail (1/4 – 1/2 in. above bottom)

Bottom of coffee can

Figure 3

6. Repeat step 5 every 1/2 to 3/4 in. (1.28 to 1.9 cm) around the can until you reach your first hole (Figure 4).

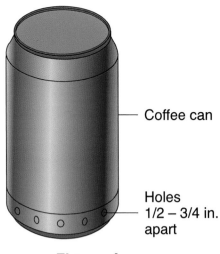

Figure 4

7. Remove all labels from the smaller can.

8. Using the can opener, completely remove the top of the can.

9. Hammer the nail into the side of the smaller can about 1/2 to 1 in. (2.56 cm) below the top of the can to create a hole (Figure 5).

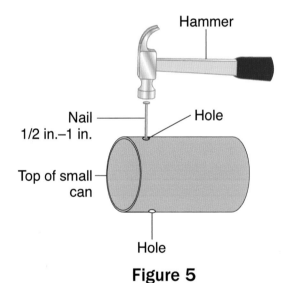

Figure 5

10. Repeat step 9 on the exact opposite side of the hole you made (Figure 5).

11. Insert the metal skewer through the 2 holes of the smaller can (Figure 6).

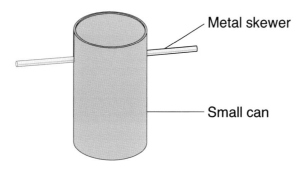

Figure 6

12. Measure 1/2 cup of water and pour it into the smaller can.

13. Wait about 1/2 hour for the water to reach room temperature.

14. Insert the thermometer into the water.

15. Record the temperature reading on your paper.

16. Remove the thermometer.

17. Place the cork/needle/peanut onto the non-flammable surface.

18. Light the peanut.

19. Quickly place the large can over the cork/needle/peanut (Figure 7).

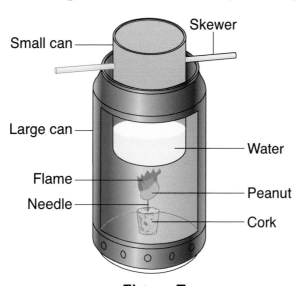

Figure 7

20. Immediately place the skewer in the small can so that the skewer rests on top of the large can, with the small can hanging inside the large can over the burning peanut (Figure 7).

21. After the peanut burns out, insert the thermometer back into the water and stir slightly.

22. Record the temperature observed on the thermometer.

 **Observations**

1. What happened to the temperature of the water?

2. Why did this occur?

3. What do you think would happen if you burned more than 1 peanut?

4. What other information would you need to calculate how much energy was released from the peanut?

5. How do we know there was stored energy in the peanut?

Our Findings

Please refer to the Our Findings appendix at the back of this volume.

Further Reading

"Energy." *The Columbia Encyclopedia*, 6th ed. 2008. Available online. URL: http://www.encyclopedia.com/doc/1E1-energy.html. Accessed June 7, 2010. Web site for children that explains the different forms of energy, including specific examples and additional links.

"Forms of Energy." Energy Kids. 2010. Available online. URL: http://www.eia.doe.gov/kids/energy.cfm?page=about_forms_of_energy-forms. Accessed June 7, 2010. Encyclopedia entry explaining the different forms of energy.

Holzner, Steven. *Physics Essentials for Dummies.* Hoboken, NJ: For Dummies, 2010. Detailed information analyzing physics concepts and types of energy.

"Potential energy." *World Encyclopedia*. 2005. Available online. URL: http://www.encyclopedia.com/doc/1O142-potentialenergy.html. Accessed June 7, 2010. Short entry defining potential energy as stored energy.

Viegas, Jennifer. *Kinetic and Potential Energy: Understanding Changes Within Physical Systems*. New York: Rosen Publishing Group, 2004. Book for young adults explaining potential and kinetic energy.

10. TESTING THE EFFECT OF HEAT ON EGG COAGULATION

Introduction

Bakers know that adding eggs to their batters help *culinary* creations reach the appropriate *texture* and *consistency*. Too many eggs, though, can take away from the flavor of the food and cause it to simply taste like the added eggs. When eggs are added to a *mixture* and that mixture is heated, the batter changes from a liquid to a *semi-solid* or *solid state*—because the *protein* in eggs *coagulates*. *Coagulation* binds ingredients together and keeps them from crumbling apart. Coagulation does not occur just in eggs and other foods but also occurs with other proteins, such as in blood *clotting*. The addition of heat speeds up the coagulation process. Heat disrupts *hydrogen* and other *bonds* as it increases the *kinetic energy* of a *substance*. The proteins in eggs *denature* and coagulate when heated.

In this experiment, you will determine the effect of heat on *thermal* coagulation of the proteins found in eggs.

Time Needed

About 2 hours

What You Need

- milk, 3 cups (about 0.75 liters [L])
- sugar, about 7 tablespoons (tbsp; 100 grams)
- 4 eggs
- salt, a tbsp (15 milliliter [ml])

- vanilla, 1 teaspoon (tsp; 5 ml)
- double boiler
- stove top
- medium-sized bowl
- fork
- oven
- oven mitts
- microwave oven
- 6 custard cups
- Pyrex® baking dish that is at least as deep as the custard cup
- sink and faucet with running water
- paper towels, a few
- stopwatch or clock
- 6 toothpicks
- paper, lined, 1 sheet
- pen or pencil

Safety Precautions

Please review and follow the safety guidelines at the beginning of this volume.

What You Do

1. Preheat the oven to 350°F.
2. Crack open 1 egg into the bowl.
3. Observe the egg yolk and egg white. Record your observations regarding the texture and consistency of the egg on the sheet of paper.
4. Slightly mix the egg with the fork.
5. Add 25 grams of sugar and a pinch of salt to the egg.

6. Mix the ingredients with the fork.

7. Heat milk in the double boiler until the milk is scalded.

8. Carefully add the hot milk to the egg mixture.

9. Fill 2 custard cups with the mixture.

10. Place the custard cups inside the baking dish.

11. Fill the baking dish with water up to the level of the custard cups (Figure 1).

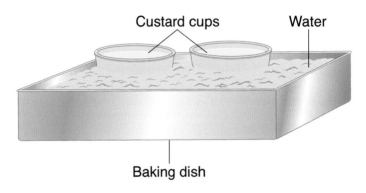

Figure 1

12. Bake until a toothpick inserted halfway in the center of the custard cup (Figure 2) comes out clean. Then remove the baking dish from the oven using oven mitts.

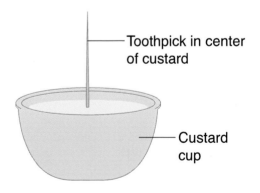

Figure 2

13. Repeat steps 1 to 12 but without adding water to the baking dish.

14. Repeat steps 1 to 12 but use 2 eggs instead of 1.

15. Remove the custards from their cups.

16. Record your observations on the data table regarding consistency (e.g., firm), texture (e.g., smooth, no holes), and flavor (e.g., "eggy")

Data Table			
Observations	With water in dish	No water in dish	2 eggs
Consistency			
Texture			
Flavor			

 Observations

1. What differences did you notice between the egg prior to cooking and the end result of your experiment?

2. Which treatment (water in the dish, no water, 2 eggs) produced the custard with the best consistency (firmness, holds its shape)? Why do you think this occurred?

3. Which treatment produced the custard with the best texture (smooth, little or no holes)? Why do think this occurred?

4. Which of the treatments contained the most protein?

5. Taste each one. Which had the best flavor and did not taste like eggs?

6. Would the eggs have hardened to the right consistency without heating? What did the heat do to the protein in the eggs?

Our Findings

Please refer to the Our Findings appendix at the back of this volume.

Further Reading

Branden, Carl, and John Tooze. *Introduction to Protein Structure.* London: Garland Science, 1999. Textbook that explains how proteins are formed and what components comprise proteins.

"Coagulation." *The Columbia Encyclopedia*, 6th ed. 2008. Available online. URL: http://www.encyclopedia.com/doc/1E1-coagulat. html. Accessed June 8, 2010. Short entry defining coagulation and providing examples of coagulation.

"Egg." Oregon State University. 2009. Available online. URL: http:// food.oregonstate.edu/learn/egg.html. Accessed June 8, 2010. Provides details about the structure of eggs and their protein content.

"Eggs." Baking Management. 2005. Available online. URL: http:// baking-management.com/rd_applications/bm_imp_8806/. Accessed June 8, 2010. Article about how eggs are used in baked goods.

Figoni, Paula. *How Baking Works: Exploring the Fundamentals of Baking Science.* Hoboken, NJ: Wiley, 2007. Explains the science behind baking, why certain ingredients are needed, and how they affect texture and consistency.

11. USING CHEMICALS TO MAKE SOAP

Introduction

We use soap for washing our skin, our dishes, our cars, and our clothing. We think of soap as a safe *substance* that keeps us and our belongings clean. However, we rarely stop to think about the fact that soap is created from *chemicals,* and, for some types of soaps, these chemicals are extremely dangerous in their original forms. Soap is actually made up of a *sodium salt* and a long chain *hydrocarbon*, or *fatty acid*. The hydrocarbons dissolve dirt and oils; the sodium salt is *ionic*, allowing the substance to be *water soluble*. Soap dissolves grease by separating the fatty *molecules* from the surface of the item being washed, surrounding each molecule with the soap and *suspending* it in water to be rinsed away. This combination allows soapy water to remove what otherwise would be considered *insoluble* matter from your skin or clothes.

In this activity, you will combine chemicals to create homemade soap.

Time Needed

90 minutes

What You Need

- lard or shortening (e.g., Crisco™), less than 1 tablespoon (tbsp; 10 grams [g])
- 6N sodium hydroxide, 1/2 ounce (oz; 15 milliliters [ml]), available from science supply stores such as Science Kit and Boreal Laboratories or Carolina Scientific Supply Company

- ethanol (ethyl alcohol), 1.7 oz (50 ml), available from science supply stores such as Science Kit and Boreal Laboratories or Carolina Scientific Supply Company

- table salt, less than 1 tbsp (about 12 g)

- water, about 2.4 oz (70 ml)

- 2 large Pyrex® beakers

- stirring rod

- vinegar, 1 bottle, for safety purposes to counteract the sodium hydroxide if it touches skin

- rubber gloves

- goggles

- hot plate

- well-ventilated work area, preferably under a fume hood

- clock or timer

Safety Precautions

Please review and follow the safety guidelines at the beginning of this volume. Adult supervision is required for this activity, as are goggles. Exercise all safety precautions while handling sodium hydroxide with rubber gloves, and avoid contact with skin or eyes. Do not breathe in the fumes. Conduct this activity in a well-ventilated area. If any sodium hydroxide splashes on the skin, rinse immediately with vinegar and seek medical attention.

What You Do

1. Add 10 g of lard or shortening to the beaker.
2. Carefully add 15 ml of the sodium hydroxide to the beaker.
3. Add 50 ml of ethanol to the beaker.
4. Place the beaker on the hotplate with low heat while stirring for about 20 to 25 minutes (Figure 1).

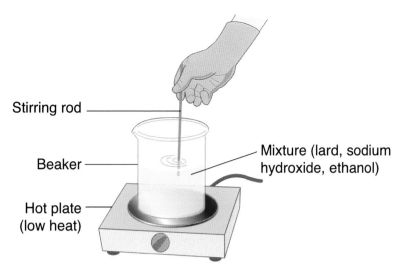

Stirring rod

Beaker

Hot plate
(low heat)

Mixture (lard, sodium
hydroxide, ethanol)

Figure 1

5. Remove the beaker from the hot plate.

6. Add 20 ml of water while stirring.

7. Allow the mixture to cool.

8. In another large beaker, combine 12 g of salt and 50 ml of water.

9. Pour the cooled contents of the first beaker into the salt-water mixture (Figure 2).

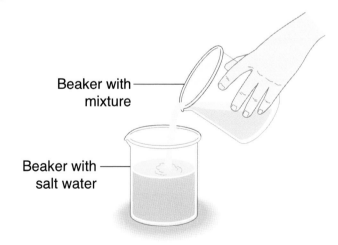

Beaker with
mixture

Beaker with
salt water

Figure 2

10. After the mixture has cooled, the solid that formed is soap.

 **Observations**

1. What differences did you notice in the consistency or state of matter of the original ingredients compared to the final product?
2. Why was lard or shortening needed to create soap?
3. Why was salt needed to produce soap?
4. What could you add to the mixture to create different-colored soaps or scented soaps?

Our Findings

Please refer to the Our Findings appendix at the back of this volume.

Further Reading

Failor, Catherine. *Making Natural Liquid Soaps*. North Adams, MA: Storey Publishing, 2000. Provides information on creating liquid soaps as opposed to solid soaps.

"Fatty Acid." *The Columbia Encyclopedia*, 6th ed. 2008. Available online. URL: http://www.encyclopedia.com/doc/1E1-fattyaci.html. Accessed June 9, 2010. Short entry about fatty acids that also contains links to related entries, such as glycerol.

Letcavage, Elizabeth. *Basic Soap Making*. Mechanicsburg, PA: Stackpole Books, 2009. For those interested in making more intricate soaps and related materials, this book provides step-by-step information.

Myers, Jack. "What Is Soap Made Of?" Highlightkids.com. 2010. Available online. URL: http://www.highlightskids.com/Science/ScienceQuestions/h1scienceQuestion13.asp. Accessed June 9, 2010. Children's Web site that explains what soap is made of.

"Soap." *The Columbia Encyclopedia*, 6th ed. 2008. Available online. URL: http://www.encyclopedia.com/doc/1E1-soap.html. Accessed June 9, 2010. This entry includes the history of soap, with explanations about how it is made.

12. USING KITCHEN CHEMISTRY TO MAKE GLUE

Introduction

Your kitchen is filled with common *chemicals*. Vinegar is an *acid*; baking soda is a *base*. All acids and bases are not safe to handle, but these two are safe. Food items containing *proteins* that can be used for experiments are milk, cheese, poultry, and meat. Some experiments that you can safely perform with items from your kitchen result in a *chemical reaction*. When a chemical reaction occurs in a *liquid*, the *solid* formed is called the *precipitate*; the liquid remaining above the solid is called the *supernate*.

In this experiment, you will combine chemicals commonly found in a kitchen to create a precipitate that can be used as glue.

Time Needed

30 minutes

What You Need

- skim milk, 1/2 cup (125 ml)
- vinegar, 1 1/2 tablespoons (25 ml)
- baking soda, 1/2 teaspoon (2 g)
- stirrer
- 2 beakers, medium or large
- funnel
- 1 filter paper

✎   water, 2 tablespoons (30 ml)

✎   hotplate

✎   oven mitts

Safety Precautions

Please review and follow the safety guidelines at the beginning of this volume. Adult supervision is recommended when using a heat source.

What You Do

1. Pour the milk into a beaker.

2. Add the vinegar to the milk.

3. Place the beaker on the hotplate and gently stir while heating until small lumps appear (Figure 1).

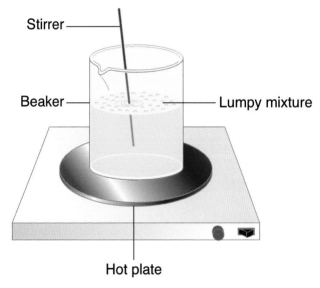

Figure 1

4. Wearing oven mitts, carefully remove the beaker from the heat.

5. Stir again until no new lumps form.

6. Place the filter paper inside the funnel (Figure 2).

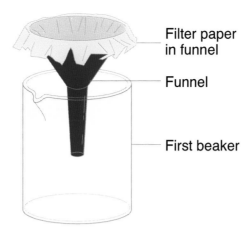

Figure 2

7. Place the funnel into the second beaker (Figure 2).

8. Pour the entire contents of the beaker with the lumpy substance into the funnel so that the liquid ends up in the second beaker.

9. Lift the filter paper out of the funnel and squeeze any liquid left through the filter paper into the beaker (Figure 3).

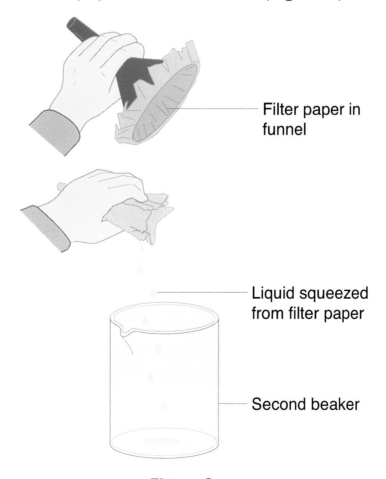

Figure 3

10. Return the solid pieces that remain in the filter paper to the first beaker.

11. Add the water to the solid pieces.

12. Stir the water and solids together.

13. Slowly add the baking soda to the water mixture, which will cause bubbles to appear, until the mixture no longer bubbles.

14. Observe the results.

 **Observations**

1. What substance was left in the beaker after mixing the solids with water and baking soda?

2. What is the relationship between the vinegar and the baking soda?

3. What did the vinegar and the heat do to the proteins in the milk?

4. How was the protein separated from the liquid?

Our Findings

Please refer to the Our Findings appendix at the back of this volume.

Further Reading

Baldwin, Carol. *Mixtures, Compounds, and Solutions*. Portsmouth, NH: Heinemann, 2004. Children's book that explains the differences between mixtures, compounds, and solutions, along with a description of their characteristics.

"Coagulation." *The Columbia Encyclopedia*, 6th ed. 2008. Available online. URL: http://www.encyclopedia.com/doc/1E1-coagulat.html. Accessed June 17, 2010. Explains how solids can be separated from liquids through coagulation.

Newmark, Ann. *Chemistry*. New York: DK Children, 2005. Illustrated book for children about chemistry and related topics.

"Precipitation." *The Columbia Encyclopedia*, 6th ed. 2008. Available online. URL: http://www.encyclopedia.com/doc/1E1-precipit1.html. Accessed June 17, 2010. Definition of precipitate, with specific examples of how precipitates form.

"Solution." *The Columbia Encyclopedia*, 6th ed. 2008. Available online. URL: http://www.encyclopedia.com. Accessed June 17, 2010. Explanation of a chemical solution and a description of the characteristics of solutions.

13. CREATING A MAGNETIC LINEAR ACCELERATOR

Introduction

Kinetic energy is the *energy* of motion; it can be transferred from one object to another, such as in a game of billiards. The player hits the cue ball; the cue ball, in turn, hits another ball; the cue ball stops and sends the other ball speeding off. An initial amount of energy is required to get a resting body in motion. This is the concept behind a *linear accelerator*. Whether scientists are testing an object, particle, or ion, a linear accelerator increases the *velocity* of the item in question using magnets, *microwaves*, or *electrons*. Linear accelerators are used for radiation therapy as well as for various types of scientific research.

In this activity, you will create a small magnetic linear accelerator and observe it in action.

Time Needed

30 minutes

What You Need

- ✎ wooden ruler with a groove down the center
- ✎ transparent tape
- ✎ scissors
- ✎ flat tabletop
- ✎ 9 small, steel balls, about 5/8 in. (1.6 cm) in diameter (available from science supply companies such as Science Kit and Boreal Laboratories or online from scitoyscatalog.com or shop.miniscience.com)

4 magnets, either rectangular or square in shape, about 3/4 to 1 in. (2 cm to 2.5 cm) wide, as strong as possible (available from science supply companies such as Science Kit and Boreal Laboratories or online from scitoyscatalog.com or shop. miniscience.com)

 large textbook or other object that can be stood on end

Safety Precautions

Please review and follow the safety guidelines at the beginning of this volume.

What You Do

1. Tape the ends of the ruler to the tabletop (Figure 1).

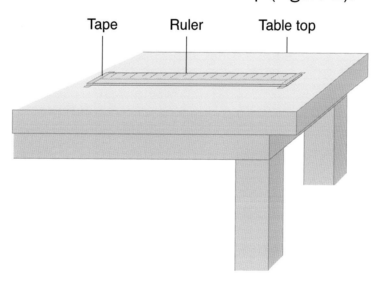

Tape   Ruler   Table top

Figure 1

2. Placing tape over the top of a magnet, tape 1 magnet at the 2.5-in. mark of the magnet (Figure 2). If the tape is too wide, trim it to fit the size of the magnet.

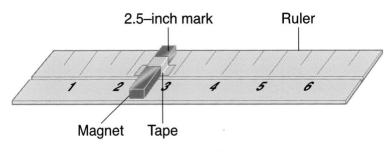

Figure 2

3. Space the other 3 magnets 2.5 in. away from each other along the ruler.

4. Repeat step 2.

5. Place 2 steel balls on the right side of each magnet (Figure 3). In the figure, the balls are larger than scale.

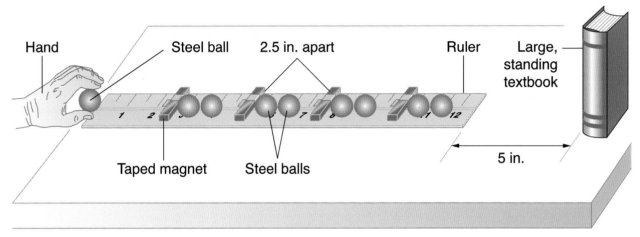

Figure 3

6. Stand up the textbook about 5 in. from the far end of the ruler (Figure 3).

7. Hold 1 steel ball to the left of the first magnet where you can just feel the pull of the magnet on the ball (Figure 3).

8. Release the ball and observe what happens.

 **Observations**

1. What happened when the ball you released hit the first magnet?
2. What happened with a ball hitting each successive magnet?
3. What did you observe about the last ball on the ruler?
4. Why did this happen? Think in terms of kinetic energy.

Our Findings

Please refer to the Our Findings appendix at the back of this volume.

Further Reading

"Linear Accelerator." Radiologyinfo.org. 2010. Available online. URL: http://www.radiologyinfo.org/en/info.cfm?pg=linac. Accessed June 19, 2010. Explains how linear accelerators are used for the treatment of cancer.

Nardo, Don. *Kinetic Energy: The Energy of Motion*. Mankato, MN: Compass Point Books, 2008. Children's book that explains the difference between potential and kinetic energy, as well as how kinetic energy is transferred to other objects.

"Particle Accelerator." *The Columbia Encyclopedia*, 6th ed. 2008. Available online. URL: http://www.encyclopedia.com/doc/1E1-partaccl.html. Accessed June 19, 2010. History and applications of particle accelerators, also known as linear accelerators.

"SLAC." Stanford.edu. 2010. Available online. URL: http://www.slac.stanford.edu/. Accessed June 19, 2010. Official Web site of the Stanford University linear accelerator, operated for the U.S. Department of Energy.

Woodford, Chris. *Energy (See for Yourself)*. New York: DK Children, 2007. Geared toward middle-schoolers, this book contains informative captioned diagrams and photographs explaining energy.

14. TESTING DETERGENTS FOR EFFECTIVENESS ON GREASE

Introduction

We wash many things: dishes, clothing, pets, and even ourselves. When we think of washing and cleaning, we think of water. We also use soap, dishwashing *detergent*, shampoo, laundry detergent, and other soap-like substances. There is actually a science behind this. Soap removes stains that plain water cannot because soap contains *emulsifiers,* which allow water and oil to mix, making it possible for grease to be lifted off the surface of the item being washed. Today, some cleaners actually contain *enzymes* to assist with the breakdown of *protein*-based stains. However, most stains we observe on a daily basis are due to dirt and grease. Various detergents claim to be the best at removing stains from clothing, while dishwashing liquids claim to be best at removing grease from dishes. Is there really a difference between the different brands?

In this experiment, you will test detergents for their effectiveness in removing a greasy stain.

Time Needed

30 minutes

What You Need

- 5 white index cards, unlined
- lipstick
- masking tape, 5 pieces
- pen

5 large, clear-plastic cups

       water, 1 tablespoon (tbsp; 15 milliliters [ml])

       5 cotton swabs

       liquid dishwashing detergent, 1 tbsp (15 ml)

       liquid hand soap, 1 tbsp

       liquid laundry detergent, 1 tbsp

       liquid laundry detergent with bleach, 1 tbsp

       measuring spoons

Safety Precautions

Please review and follow the safety guidelines at the beginning of this volume.

What You Do

1. Label each of 5 cups, using the masking tape and pen, with the following names: Water, Dishwashing detergent, Hand soap, Laundry detergent, and Laundry detergent with bleach (Figure 1).

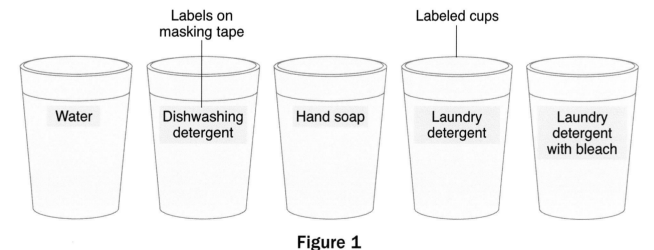

Figure 1

2. Add 1 tbsp of water to the cup labeled "Water."

3. Add 1 tbsp of each type of detergent and soap being tested to each of the other 4 cups.

4. Label the top of each index card with the corresponding names written on the cups (Figure 2).

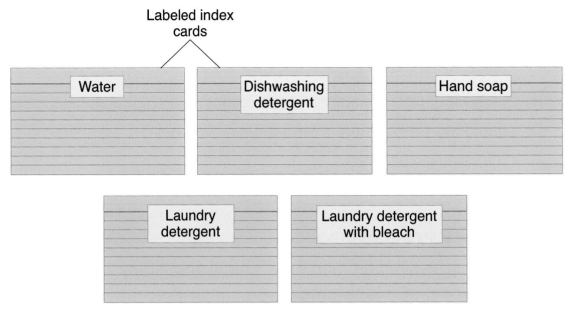

Figure 2

5. On the card labeled "Water," draw a circle in lipstick and fill it in with more lipstick to make a circle about the size of a quarter (Figure 3).

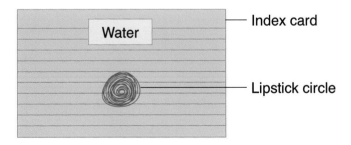

Figure 3

6. Dip the end of 1 cotton swab into the cup labeled "Water," then lay the wet end of the cotton swab on the lipstick circle of the index card labeled "Water."

7. Keeping the swab horizontal and the wet end against the lipstick circle, move the wet end of the swab in a circular motion over the lipstick 20 times (Figure 4).

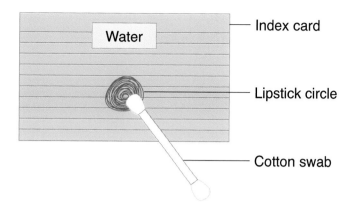

Figure 5

8. Lay the swab down next to the circle on the index card (Figure 5).

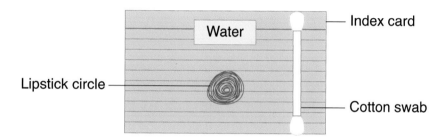

Figure 5

9. Repeat steps 6 to 8 for each of the other substances and corresponding index cards.

10. Observe the lipstick on the index cards and the cotton swabs.

 **Observations**

1. What did you notice about the cotton swab that was dipped in:
    a. Water?
    b. Dishwashing detergent?
    c. Hand soap?
    d. Laundry detergent?
    e. Laundry detergent with bleach?

2. What did you notice about the lipstick circles on the index cards that were treated with:

   a. Water?

   b. Dishwashing detergent?

   c. Hand soap?

   d. Laundry detergent?

   e. Laundry detergent with bleach?

3. Which do you think was most effective at removing the lipstick? Which was least effective?

4. Why do we use detergent or soap instead of just water for washing dishes, clothing, and ourselves?

Our Findings

Please refer to the Our Findings appendix at the back of this volume.

Further Reading

"Colloid." *The Columbia Encyclopedia*, 6th ed. 2008. Available online. URL: http://www.encyclopedia.com/doc/1E1-colloid.html. Accessed June 19, 2010. Explains the relationships between emulsifiers and colloids.

"Detergent." *The Columbia Encyclopedia*, 6th ed. 2008. Available online. URL: http://www.encyclopedia.com/doc/1E1-detergen.html. Accessed June 19, 2010. Short explanation of the science behind detergents.

"Eutrophication." *The Columbia Encyclopedia*, 6th ed. 2008. Available online. URL: http://www.encyclopedia.com/doc/1E1-eutrophi.html. Accessed June 19, 2010. Describes the side effect that can occur to waterways where too much detergent has been dumped.

Rogers, Kirsteen, Laura Howell, Alastair Smith, Phillip Clarke, and Corinne Henderson. *The Usborne Science Encyclopedia*. Thornton, CO: Usborne Books, 2009. Comprehensive children's science encyclopedia.

Wertheim, Jane. *The Illustrated Dictionary of Chemistry*. Thornton, CO: Usborne Books, 2000. Illustrated children's dictionary of chemistry terms.

15. CREATING AND OBSERVING ANTI-BUBBLES

Introduction

We have all heard of, seen, or even made bubbles. But many people are not aware of the existence of *anti-bubbles*, which are the opposite of bubbles. Bubbles are air surrounded by a thin coat of *liquid*, while anti-bubbles form in liquid with a thin film of air surrounding the *fluid*. In other words, there is liquid both inside the anti-bubble and outside of it, separated by a thin layer of air. Since air bubbles are lighter than anti-bubbles, anti-bubbles take longer to rise to the surface, and if the liquid inside is heavier than the liquid outside the anti-bubble, it can actually sink.

In this activity, you will create anti-bubbles and observe their *properties*.

Time Needed

25 minutes

What You Need

✎ kitchen sink with flowing water

✎ large, clean, glass jar

✎ dishwashing liquid (e.g., Dawn® or Palmolive®), about 1/3 to 1/2 tablespoons (5–10 milliliters [ml])

✎ clean, empty, glue bottle, washed thoroughly (e.g., Elmer's® glue)

✎ long stirrer

✎ comb

✎ 5 to 10 drops of red food coloring

Safety Precautions

Please review and follow the safety guidelines at the beginning of this volume.

What You Do

1. Place the glass jar inside the sink under the faucet.
2. Turn on the faucet and fill the glass jar, then allow the water to continue to overfill the jar. Leave the faucet running on low (Figure 1).

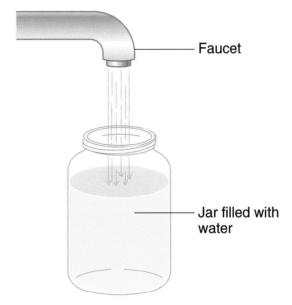

Figure 1

3. Add about 5 to 10 ml of dishwashing liquid into the jar.
4. Stir the water and dishwashing liquid in the jar.
5. Take the top off the empty glue bottle and fill the bottle with the soapy water from the jar.
6. Add 5 to 10 drops of red food coloring to the glue bottle.
7. Gently swish the glue bottle to evenly spread the coloring.
8. Replace the top of the glue bottle.

9. Squirt some globules of soapy water from the glue bottle onto the top of the water in the jar (Figure 2).

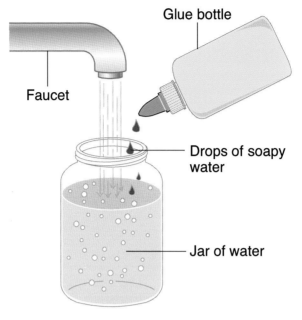

Figure 2

10. Observe the action of the globules.

11. Comb your hair.

12. Wave the comb, now charged with static electricity, near the globules of soapy water that are in the jar (Figure 3).

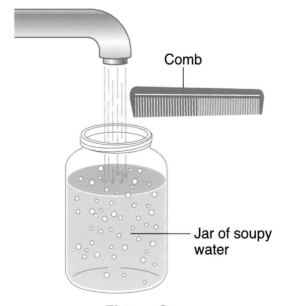

Figure 3

13. Turn the glue bottle upside down and hold it just above the water surface of the jar (Figure 4).

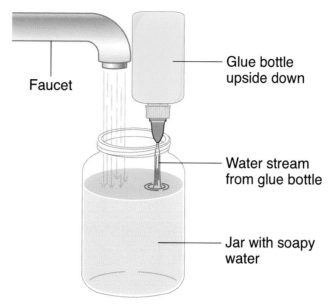

Faucet

Glue bottle
upside down

Water stream
from glue bottle

Jar with soapy
water

Figure 4

14. Gently squeeze the bottle just enough to create a globule of water (Figure 4).

15. Immediately squeeze the bottle stronger, forcing a stream of water through the globule.

16. Repeat steps 14 and 15 four more times.

17. Observe the anti-bubbles that form.

 **Observations**

1. What is the difference between a bubble and an anti-bubble?

2. What was the purpose in adding red food coloring to the glue bottle?

3. What happened to the globules when you exposed them to static electricity with the comb? Why did this happen?

Our Findings

Please refer to the Our Findings appendix at the back of this volume.

Further Reading

"Antibubbles." *Antibubbles.org*. 2010. Available online. URL: http://www.antibubble.org/. Accessed June 13, 2010. With text and diagrams, this article is about the formation of anti-bubbles and their properties, expressed in simple terms.

"Bubble Questions." Bubbles.org. 2010. Available online. URL: http://bubbles.org/html/questions/questions.htm. Accessed June 13, 2010. Children's Web site with interesting facts about bubbles and related activities.

Clift, R., J. R. Grace, and M. E. Weber. *Bubbles, Drops, and Particles*. Mineola, NY: Dover Publications, 2005. Advanced text about the physics behind bubbles and water droplets.

Isenberg, Cyril. *The Science of Soap Films and Soap Bubbles*. Mineola, NY: Dover Publications, 1992. Advanced text about the science behind soap bubbles, along with numerous photographs.

Stein, David. *How to Make Monstrous, Huge, Unbelievably Big Bubbles*. Palo Alto, CA: Klutz, 2005. All-inclusive book with information ranging from the history of bubbles to how to make gigantic bubbles, along with color photographs.

16. USING STEAM TO POWER A BOAT

Introduction

After they were introduced in the 18th century, *steamboats* replaced sailboats in the United States for shipping and trade back in the 19th century. Later, steam-driven engines were replaced by gas *turbines*. However, a few steamboats can still be found today on major rivers of the United States. In most cases, steamboats use the steam to drive *paddle wheels*. The concept of using steam to *propel* a boat is actually not that far off from the idea of rocket *propulsion*. If a great enough *force* is generated, an equal and opposite reaction occurs. The force created by the steam pushes the boat forward, while the explosion of a *combustion* engine of a rocket pushes it up and away from *gravity*.

In this activity, you will simulate the action of a steamboat and observe how steam can be used to propel an object.

Time Needed

60 minutes

What You Need

- ✎ empty metal tube, such as those used to contain a cigar
- ✎ cork, to fit the opening of the metal tube
- ✎ 2 thin-wire hangers
- ✎ 2 food-warmer candles in metal cups
- ✎ balsa wood, 4 in. by 8 in. (10 cm by 20 cm), 1/2 in. (1.3 cm) thick

✎   masking tape, 2 pieces

✎   hammer

✎   3 nails about 1 in. (2.5 cm) to 1 1/2 in. (about 4 cm) long

✎   long matches, 1 or 2

✎   ruler

✎   pliers

✎   wire cutter

✎   whittling tool or carving knife

✎   hot (near-boiling) water, enough to fill tube

✎   bathtub filled halfway with water

Safety Precautions

Please review and follow the safety guidelines at the beginning of this volume. Adult supervision is required. Exercise caution when using sharp tools and handling sharp objects. Exercise caution when working with lighted candles or handling hot liquids.

What You Do

1. Poke a hole through the cork with a nail and then remove the nail (Figure 1).

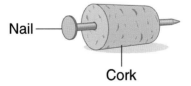

Nail

Cork

Figure 1

2. Untwist the wire hangers to create two 18-in. wires. If necessary, cut to size with a wire cutter.

3. About 1 in. from one end of the metal tube, twist the center of one of the wires around it and tighten in place with pliers to prevent the tube from slipping out of the wire (Figure 2).

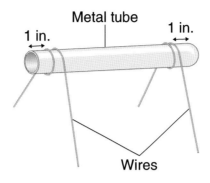

Figure 2

4. Repeat step 3 with the other wire on the other end of the metal tube.

5. Carve a boat shape out of the balsa wood so it looks like the shape in Figure 3.

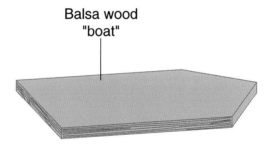

Figure 3

6. Hammer 1 nail, centered, about 1 in. from one end of the boat so that the nail extends past the wood (Figure 4).

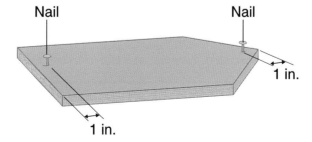

Figure 4

7. Repeat step 6 on the other end of the boat.

8. Make 2 small loops of masking tape.

9. Stick a loop under each metal cup with candle.

10. Stick the metal cups with the candles in them to the "boat," about 1 1/2 in. from each end of the boat (Figure 5).

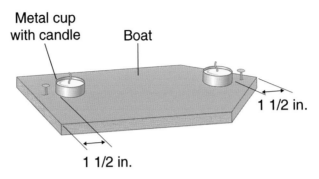

Figure 5

11. Holding the metal tube about 1/2 in. above the candles, wrap both ends of each wire around and under the boat (Figure 6).

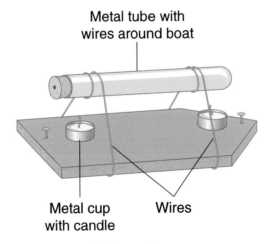

Figure 6

12. Tighten the wires under the boat so that they lay as flat as possible. If necessary, cut off excess wire with a wire cutter.

13. Carefully fill the metal tube about 3/4 full with hot water and seal it with the cork. Water will drip from holes in the tube made by the nails.

14. Place your boat into the bathtub that is half-filled with water.

15. Carefully light both candles.

16. Observe what happens.

 **Observations**

1. What happened to the boat?

2. Why was it necessary to poke a hole in the cork?

3. What was the benefit of using hot water as opposed to cold water in the tube?

4. How does this also model rocket propulsion?

Our Findings

Please refer to the Our Findings appendix at the back of this volume.

Further Reading

Potter, Jerry. *The Sultana Tragedy: America's Greatest Maritime Disaster*. Gretna, LA: Pelican Publishing, 1992. Historical look at one of the worst tragedies in America, when 1,800 Union veterans of the Civil War were killed in a steamboat explosion.

O'Donnell, Ed. *Ship Ablaze: The Tragedy of the Steamboat General Slocum*. New York: Broadway, 2004. Recounts the disaster of a steamboat tragedy that claimed over 1,000 lives.

"Steamboating the Rivers." Steamboats.org. 2010. Available online. URL: http://www.steamboats.org/index.php. Accessed June 15, 2010. Web site about the remaining steamboats found on America's rivers.

"Steamboats." *Gale Encyclopedia of U.S. Economic History*. 2000. Available online. URL: http://www.encyclopedia.com/doc/1G2-3406400896.html. Accessed June 15, 2010. Detailed article about the history of steamboat engines.

"Welcome to the Beginner's Guide to Propulsion." NASA.gov. 2008. Available online. URL: http://www.grc.nasa.gov/WWW/K-12/airplane/bgp.html. Accessed June 15, 2010. Official NASA Web site with links to information for students and teachers about how propulsion works.

17. DETECTING INFRARED RADIATION

Introduction

Sir Frederick William Herschel (1728–1822), a German-born *astronomer* who *emigrated* from Germany to England, was known for building *telescopes* and for his discovery of the planet Uranus. In the year 1800, he made an important discovery. He tested the amount of heat in the different colors of the *visible-light spectrum* and discovered that there was more heat generated just past the red portion of the spectrum. By doing this, he *inadvertently* discovered *infrared radiation*. Today, we know that infrared radiation is electromagnetic radiation with a *wavelength* longer than that of visible light and has many applications for technological use.

In this activity, you will recreate Herschel's experiment and verify the existence of infrared radiation.

Time Needed

30 minutes

What You Need

- ✎ 3 alcohol thermometers
- ✎ equilateral glass prism
- ✎ empty cardboard box with no lid, such as from a case of paper
- ✎ white paper, unlined, 1 sheet
- ✎ black paint
- ✎ small paintbrush

✎   sunny outdoor area

✎   transparent tape

✎   a few rocks or bricks

✎   timer or clock

✎   pen or pencil

✎   lined paper, 1 sheet

Safety Precautions

Please review and follow the safety guidelines at the beginning of this volume.

What You Do

1. Paint the bulbs of all 3 thermometers black (Figure 1). Allow them to dry.

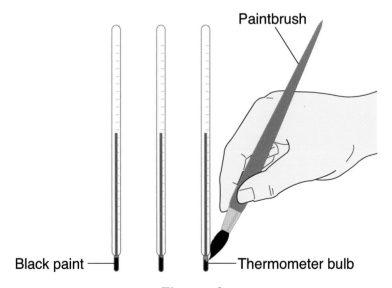

Figure 1

2. Lay the sheet of white paper down inside the box.
3. Tape the prism inside the top edge of a side of the box (Figure 2).

Prism taped inside   Cardboard box
top edge

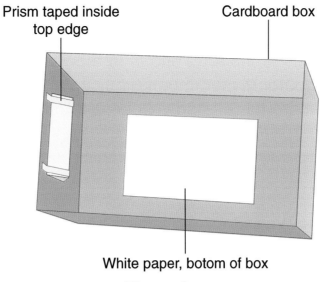

White paper, botom of box

Figure 2

4. If the spectrum of visible light is not appearing clearly on the white sheet of paper inside the box, tilt the box until the prism appears, and place rocks or bricks underneath the box to hold the correct angle (Figure 3).

Visible-light spectrum
on white paper

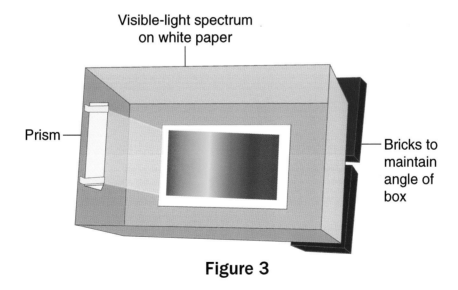

Prism

Bricks to
maintain
angle of
box

Figure 3

5. Place the thermometers inside the box where the light is shaded.

6. After 5 minutes, record the temperatures shown on the thermometers.

7. Move the thermometers until they are directly in the path of the light spectrum so that the bulb of one thermometer is in the blue part of the spectrum, one is in the yellow part, and the last thermometer is just immediately past the red part of the spectrum where there is no visible light (Figure 4).

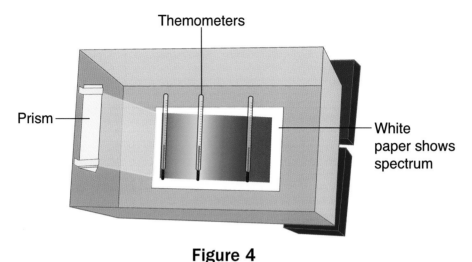

Themometers

Prism

White
paper shows
spectrum

Figure 4

8. After 5 minutes, record the temperatures shown on the thermometers.

 **Observations**

1. What were the initial thermometer readings?
2. What were the thermometer readings after they were moved to positions within the spectrum?
3. Which part of the spectrum gave the highest temperature reading? What did this prove?

Our Findings

Please refer to the Our Findings appendix at the back of this volume.

Further Reading

Burnie, David. *Eyewitness: Light*. New York, DK Children, 1999. A book for students in grades 6 and up that provides a wealth of information, with illustrations on a variety of topics related to the electromagnetic spectrum.

"The Electromagnetic Spectrum." Nasa.gov. 2007. Available online. URL: http://science.hq.nasa.gov/kids/imagers/ems/infrared. html. Accessed June 12, 2010. Information for children from NASA that explains infrared and other portions of the electromagnetic spectrum.

Gould, Alan, and Stephen Pompea. *Invisible Universe: The Electromagnetic Spectrum From Radio Waves to Gamma Rays*. Berkeley, CA: LHS Gems, 2002. Produced in conjunction with NASA, this book is geared toward middle-schoolers and introduces students to the electromagnetic spectrum and invisible light.

"Infrared Radiation." *The Columbia Encyclopedia*, 6th ed. 2008. Available online. URL: http://www.encyclopedia.com/doc/1E1-infrared.html. Accessed June 12, 2010. Discusses infrared radiation, its discovery, and its applications.

"Spectrum." *The Columbia Encyclopedia*, 6th ed. 2008. Available online. URL: http://www.encyclopedia.com/doc/1E1-spectrum.html. Accessed June 12, 2010. Explains the different parts of the light spectrum along with explanations of related topics.

18. DETERMINING WHAT COLOR OF LIGHT SHINES BRIGHTEST THROUGH FOG

Introduction

Fog is often an *integral* part of horror movies because fog *obscures* vision and makes it difficult to see far ahead or behind. But fog is basically just a cloud that is touching the ground. Fog occurs when the air is *supersaturated* with *water vapor* so that the water *precipitates* in the form of a light mist. When you are driving in fog, car lights are essential so that other cars can see you and you can see what is ahead of you. However, light has its own *properties*, such as *intensity*, *frequency*, and *wavelength*. There are various colors of light; some may appear brighter in a fog than others, depending on the properties of light.

In this experiment, you will combine *meteorology* with *optics* by using a *light meter* to test the brightness of various colored lights for their effectiveness in shining through fog.

Time Needed

35 minutes

What You Need

- ✎ flashlight with fresh batteries
- ✎ glass jar with no label
- ✎ water, enough to fill the jar
- ✎ milk, 2 teaspoons (10 ml)
- ✎ long spoon for stirring

cellophane squares, 4 in. (about 10 cm) by 4 in., in each of the following colors: blue, red, purple, green, orange, and yellow

 light meter, available from electronic stores such as Radio Shack, Best Buy, or from camera supply stores

 darkened room

 pen or pencil

 transparent tape, a few pieces

Safety Precautions

Please review and follow the safety guidelines at the beginning of this volume.

What You Do

1. Fill the jar with water.
2. Add the milk to the water.
3. Stir the water and milk to form a cloudy liquid.
4. Wrap the blue cellophane square around the front of the flashlight. If necessary, tape the edges to the flashlight to hold the cellophane in place (Figure 1).

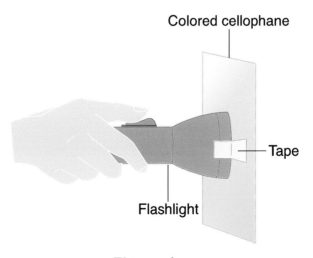

Figure 1

5. Place the flashlight behind the jar.

6. Turn on the flashlight.

7. Darken the room but leave the flashlight turned on.

8. Hold the light meter on the side of the jar opposite from the flashlight (Figure 2).

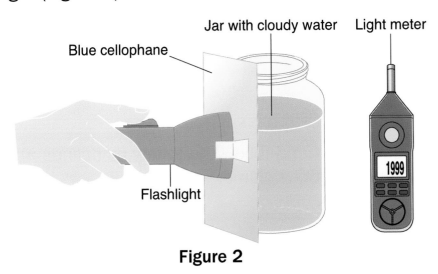

Figure 2

9. Record on the data table the intensity of the light (usually measured in lumens) measured by the light meter.

10. Repeat steps 3 to 9 with the other colors of cellophane.

Data Table	
Color	**Brightness**
blue	
red	
purple	
green	
orange	
yellow	

 **Observations**

1. Which color had the highest reading on the light meter?
2. Which had the lowest?
3. Why was milk added to the water?
4. How might this information be useful for enhancing safety during a thick fog?

Our Findings

Please refer to the Our Findings appendix at the back of this volume.

Further Reading

Dunlop, Storm. *The Weather Identification Handbook*. Guilford, CT: Lyons Press, 2003. Color photographs and diagrams highlight this book that helps identify weather patterns.

"Fog." *The Columbia Encyclopedia*, 6th ed. 2008. Available online. URL: http://www.encyclopedia.com/doc/1E1-fog.html. Accessed June 10, 2010. Explanation of how fog forms as a meteorological phenomenon.

Freudenrich, Craig. "How Light Works." Howstuffworks.com. 2010. Available online. URL: http://www.howstuffworks.com/light.htm. Accessed June 10, 2010. Explains light frequencies and how light travels.

Pasachoff, Jay. *Sound and Light*. Upper Saddle River, NJ: Pearson Prentice Hall, 2004. Explanations for children and teens regarding sound waves and light as both particles and waves.

"Types of Light." Physics4kids.com. 2010. Available online. URL: http://www.physics4kids.com/files/light_intro.html. Accessed June 10, 2010. Discusses electromagnetic radiation in terms that children can understand.

19. MODELING A NUCLEAR REACTION

Introduction

For many decades, people have explored alternative sources of energy. One such source is *nuclear fission*. In a *nuclear reactor*, *uranium-235* (U-235) is used as part of a *chain reaction* that releases large amounts of energy. In simple terms, 2 *neutrons* from U-235 are split off. Each of these neutrons then goes on to hit other U-235 *atoms*, Each of those atoms is split, releasing 2 neutrons that continue on in a chain reaction of hitting other U-235 atoms, splitting them and releasing more neutrons. However, controls must be put into place to prevent chain reactions from going on forever, so reactors usually contain *control rod*s made of *cadmium* or *boron*, both *elements* that absorb neutrons. Once the control rod is placed between uranium atoms, the number of neutrons generated is reduced.

In this activity, you will simulate a chain reaction like that of uranium-235, as well as learn how a control rod works.

Time Needed

25 minutes

What You Need

- ✎ ruler
- ✎ large, flat surface
- ✎ 35 dominoes

Safety Precautions

Please review and follow the safety guidelines at the beginning of this volume.

What You Do

1. Standing each domino vertically, arrange 10 dominoes in a straight line with about 3/4 in. between each one (Figure 1).

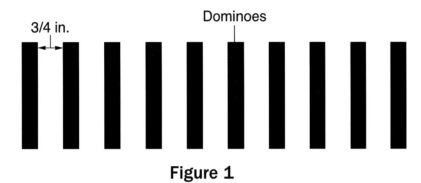

3/4 in.

Dominoes

Figure 1

2. Repeat step 1 about a foot away from the first row of dominoes to form a second line of 10 dominoes.

3. Arrange 15 dominoes in the pattern shown in Figure 2.

Top view of domino pattern modeling nuclear fission

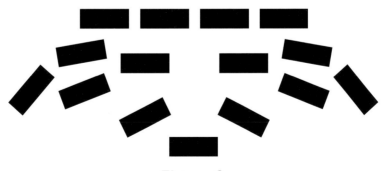

Figure 2

4. Knock over the single domino that stands at the front of the dominoes you arranged according to Figure 2.

5. Observe what happens.

6. Knock over the first domino in one of the lines of 10 dominoes you set up.

7. Observe what happens.

8. Place the ruler in the center of the second line of 10 dominoes (Figure 3).

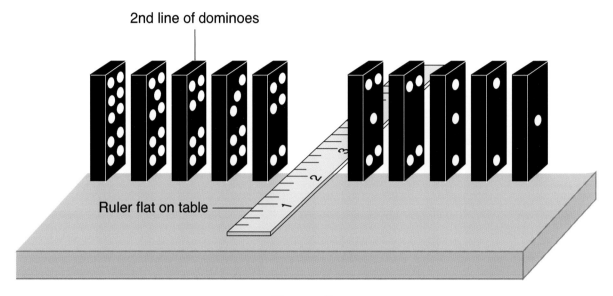

Figure 3

9. Knock over the first domino.

10. Observe what happens.

 **Observations**

1. How does the pattern shown in Figure 2 model the nuclear fission reaction of uranium-235?

2. What differences did you notice in the way the dominoes fell in the 2 straight lines when you knocked over the first domino in each line?

3. What did the ruler represent in this simulation?

Our Findings

Please refer to the Our Findings appendix at the back of this volume.

Further Reading

Alexievich, Svetlana. *Voices from Chernobyl: The Oral History of Natural Disaster*. New York: Picador, 2006. First-hand accounts of the worst nuclear reactor disaster in history, which occurred in Ukraine.

Brian, Marshall, and Robert Lamb. "How Nuclear Power Works." Howstuffworks.com. 2010. Available online. URL: http://science. howstuffworks.com/nuclear-power1.htm. Accessed June 10, 2010. Explains nuclear fission and the radiation that is emitted during the process.

"Nuclear Energy." *The Columbia Encyclopedia*, 6th ed. 2008. Available online. URL: http://www.encyclopedia.com/doc/1E1-nuclener.html. Accessed June 10, 2010. Explains nuclear energy and the process for releasing the energy stored in atoms.

"Nuclear Reactor." *The Columbia Encyclopedia*, 6th ed. 2008. Available online. URL: http://www.encyclopedia.com. Accessed June 10, 2010. Discusses nuclear energy and the role of nuclear reactors.

Walker, J. Samuel. *Three-Mile Island: A Nuclear Crisis in Historical Perspective*. Berkeley, CA: University of California Press, 2006. Detailed account of the nuclear accident that occurred at a nuclear power plant and the implications of using nuclear power as a resource.

20. CREATING A HOLOGRAM

Introduction

Holographic images, or *holograms*, are *photographic* images that are *3-dimensional*. Holograms have this appearance because they are 2 *two-dimensional* images taken from different angles and superimposed over each other. *Lasers* (an *acronym* for "light amplification by simulated emission of radiation") are used to ensure that the correct *wavelength* of light is used to create the image. The object of the image being created is placed under a *photographic plate*. Two lasers are beamed through *diffusers*, one from the side of the object and the other directly through the photographic plate above the object. The 2 beams of light leave an image on the photographic plate from 2 different perspectives, creating a hologram.

In this activity, you will not need a laser to make a hologram. Instead, you will create a simulated hologram with the same 3-dimensional effect of lasers but drawn by hand.

Time Needed

45 to 60 minutes

What You Need

- ✎ Plexiglas® or clear acrylic, at least 8 in. by 8 in. (51 cm by 51 cm)
- ✎ drafting compass with metal point for each end (available at art supply stores like Aaron Brothers) or a dividing compass with sharp points at each end
- ✎ ruler

✎   black permanent marker

✎   black paper, 1 sheet

✎   area with bright sunlight

Safety Precautions

Please review and follow the safety guidelines at the beginning of this volume.

What You Do

1. Write the first initial of your first name (e.g., A) with the marker on the Plexiglas® about 1/2 in. from the bottom and 2 1/2 in. from the left side. The letter you draw should be about 1 in. to 1 1/2 in. tall (Figure 1).

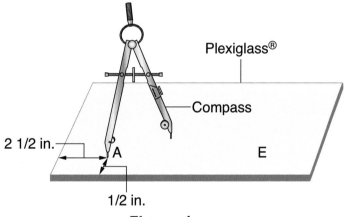

Figure 1

2. Write the first initial of your last name (e.g., E) with the marker on the Plexiglas® about 1/2 in. from the bottom and 2 1/2 in. from the right side. The letter you draw should be about 1 in. to 1 1/2 in. tall (Figure 1).

3. Make sure the compass has a sharp metal point (not a pencil) at each end.

4. Adjust the compass so that the points are about 2 in. apart (Figure 2).

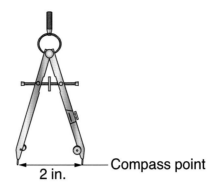

2 in. ── Compass point

Figure 2

5. Place 1 point at the bottom-left side of your first initial.

6. Lightly scratch an arc about 2 in. above that point by moving the compass back and forth and having the other point of the compass scrape across the Plexiglas® (Figure 3).

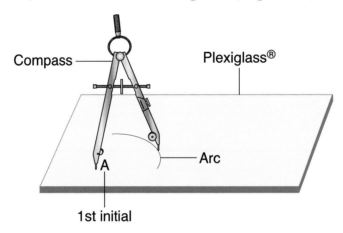

Compass ──

Plexiglass®

── Arc

A

1st initial

Figure 3

7. Move the stationary compass point about 1/8 in. over from where you were holding it, making sure it is still on the letter you drew.

8. Repeat step 6.

9. Continue to repeat steps 7 and 8 until you have multiple arcs scratched into the Plexiglas® from as many points as possible along the letter you drew.

10. Repeat steps 5 to 9 for the initial of your last name.

11. Hold the Plexiglas® horizontally, about chest high, while facing the Sun, with the letters you drew close to your body and the scratches away from your body.

12. Observe the scratches you made while tilting the Plexiglas® until you catch the sunlight just right and see your initials embedded in the Plexiglas®—in the scratches you made 2 in. above them. If you cannot see them, try holding a sheet of black paper under the Plexiglas® and repeating steps 11 and 12.

13. Turn over the Plexiglas® and repeat steps 11 and 12. You should be able to observe your initials where you made the scratches floating above the Plexiglas.®

 **Observations**

1. Were you able to see your simulated hologram?
2. Where did the hologram appear to be?
3. How are holograms typically made?
4. What other shapes could you recreate as a hologram?

Our Findings

Please refer to the Our Findings appendix at the back of this volume.

Further Reading

Bone, Jan. *Opportunities in Laser Technology*. New York: McGraw-Hill, 2008. Information about careers in the field of laser technology, including creating holograms.

DeFreitas, Frank. Holoworld.com. 2010. Available online. URL: http://www.holoworld.com/holo/kids.html. Accessed June 20, 2010. Explanation in simple terms for children about how holograms are created.

"Hologram and Holography." *UXL Encyclopedia of Science*. 2002. Available online. URL: http://www.encyclopedia.com/doc/1G2-3438100353.html. Accessed June 20, 2010. Scientific explanation of how holograms are created.

Kasper, Joseph, and Steven Feller. *The Complete Book of Holograms*. Mineola, NY: Dover Publication, 2001. A book for young adults explaining how holographic images are created. Includes photographs.

Royal Photographic Art Gallery. 2010. Available online. URL: http://www.holograms.bc.ca/index.htm. Accessed June 20, 2010. A Web site of a large hologram gallery located in Canada that includes text and images.

Scope and Sequence Chart

This chart is aligned with the National Science Content Standards. Each state may have its own specific content standards, so please refer to your local and state content standards for additional information. As always, adult supervision is recommended (or required in some instances), and discretion should be used in selecting experiments appropriate for each age group or individual children.

Standard	Experiments
Unifying Concepts and Processes	All
Science as Inquiry	All
Physical Science	
Properties of objects and materials	1, 2, 3, 4, 6, 7, 10, 11, 12, 14, 15, 20
Properties and changes of properties in matter	1, 2, 3, 4, 6, 7, 10, 11, 12, 14, 15, 20
Position and motion of objects	5, 6, 13
Motions and forces	5, 13, 16, 19
Light, heat, electricity, and magnetism	1, 8, 9, 10, 16, 17, 18, 20
Transfer of energy	2, 5, 8, 9, 10, 16, 19
Life Science	
Structure and function in living systems	
Life cycles of organisms	
Reproduction and heredity	
Regulation and behavior	

Organisms and environments	6, 8
Populations and ecosystems	
Diversity and adaptations of organisms	
Earth Science	
Properties of Earth materials	2, 4, 19
Structure of the Earth system	
Objects in the sky	
Changes in Earth and sky	
Earth's history	
Earth in the solar system	
Science and Technology	
Science in Personal and Social Perspectives	
Personal health	
Characteristics and changes in populations	
Types of resources	
Changes in environments	
Science and technology in local challenges	3, 14
Populations, resources, and environments	
Natural hazards	
Risks and benefits	
Science and technology in society	19
History and Nature of Science	All

Grade Level

Setting

The experiments are classified by materials and equipment use as follows:

- Those under SCHOOL LABORATORY involve materials and equipment found only in science laboratories. Those under SCHOOL LABORATORY must be carried out there under the supervision of the teacher or another adult.

- Those under HOME involve household or everyday materials. Some of these can be done at home, but call for supervision.

- The experiments classified under OUTDOORS may be done at the school or at the home, but require access to outdoor areas and call for supervision.

SCHOOL LABORATORY

All experiments except 16—Using Steam to Power a Boat—may also be performed in a laboratory.

HOME

1. Testing Items With a Black Light
2. Making Bath Fizzers
3. Testing Liquids for Use in Plaster
4. Creating a Geode
5. Throwing a Curveball
6. Diffusion Through a Balloon
7. Testing the Dissolution Rate of Lactase
8. Exothermic and Endothermic Reactions
9. Examining the Energy in a Peanut
10. Testing the Effect of Heat on Egg Coagulation
11. Using Chemicals to Make Soap
12. Using Kitchen Chemistry to Make Glue

OUTDOORS

Our Findings

1. TESTING ITEMS WITH A BLACK LIGHT

1. Yes, they all glowed.

2. Yes, they all glowed with the same color because they all were exposed to the same UV light.

3. Fluorescent objects absorb ultraviolet light, then immediately emit it.

2. MAKING BATH FIZZERS

1. The ball fizzed in the water.

2. The citric acid, baking soda, and water are reacting.

3. Carbon dioxide is being produced and released.

4. Answers will vary but may include changing the fragrance or adding food coloring.

3. TESTING LIQUIDS FOR USE IN PLASTER

1. Water worked best for the plaster.

2. Answers may vary, but it is likely to be the vinegar.

3. Answers may vary but should include: The plaster must be hardened to the right consistency or it will crumble, crack, or fall apart. It may not dry completely, either.

4. The chemical reaction takes place between the plaster mix and the liquid.

4. CREATING A GEODE

1. Crystals formed.

2. No, the crystals were different colors.

3. Answers may vary but could include salt water and sugar water.

4. Minerals in groundwater that has seeped into cracks in hardened lava form crystals inside rock layers.

5. THROWING A CURVEBALL

1. Yes, there was a difference.

2. The ball should have followed a curved path.

3. Since the ball is moving forward even as it is spinning, on one side of the ball the boundary layer is moving in the same direction as the air flowing around the ball. But on the other side, the boundary layer is moving in the opposite direction of the air flow. Because the two layers of air are moving in opposite directions, the air stream is slowed down, while on the other side both are moving in the same direction, so the air stream moves faster, causing the ball to move either to the right or left.

4. Answers will vary but may include pitching a softball or baseball.

6. DIFFUSION OF MOLECULES THROUGH A BALLOON

1. Answers will vary.

2. If you can smell them inside the cup, then they diffused into the cup.

3. Because the smell was transferred to the cup and the smell is due to the molecules of the item diffusing through the balloon to the cup.

4. A balloon is not completely solid; it has tiny openings we may not see with the naked eye.

7. TESTING THE DISSOLUTION RATE OF LACTASE

1. It was conducted at that temperature because that is normal human body temperature, and therefore would simulate conditions in the human body.

2. Answers will vary.

3. If it dissolved faster, it might provide faster relief.

4. Answers will vary depending on results of the experiment.

5. Answers will vary but are likely to be based on which brand dissolved the fastest.

8. EXOTHERMIC AND ENDOTHERMIC REACTIONS

1. The hydrogen peroxide and yeast reaction was exothermic because the temperature rose.

2. The baking soda and vinegar was the endothermic reaction because the temperature decreased.

3. The hydrogen peroxide and yeast reaction released energy.

4. The vinegar and baking soda reaction absorbed energy.

9. EXAMINING THE ENERGY IN A PEANUT

1. The temperature increased.

2. Energy was released from the peanut.

3. The temperature would rise more.

4. Answers will vary but may include calculating the mass of the peanut.

5. We know because the energy released heated the water.

10. TESTING THE EFFECT OF HEAT ON EGG COAGULATION

1. Prior to heating it was a liquid; the "white" of the egg was clear. After heating, it was all solid and the white appeared white.

2. Answers will vary but is likely to be the one with 2 eggs.

3. Answers will vary but is likely to be the one where water was used so that the temperature for cooking increased in a smooth manner.

4. The treatment that contained 2 eggs.

5. Answers will vary but is likely to be either of the treatments that used 1 egg.

6. No, they would not have hardened. Heating causes the protein in eggs to denature and coagulate.

11. USING CHEMICALS TO MAKE SOAP

1. The original ingredients were mainly liquids, but the product was a solid.

2. Soap is actually made up of a sodium salt and a fatty acid that dissolves dirt and oils.

3. The salt makes it water soluble.

4. Answers will vary but may include fragrance oils and food coloring.

12. USING KITCHEN CHEMISTRY TO MAKE GLUE

1. Water is left behind.

2. Vinegar is an acid and baking soda is a base.

3. They denatured the proteins and made them coagulate.

4. It formed a precipitate so was able to be separated from the liquid.

13. CREATING A MAGNETIC LINEAR ACCELERATOR

1. The momentum was passed on to the balls that were on the other side of the magnet.

2. As each ball hit each successive magnet, the movement of the balls increased in speed and passed along the momentum to the next one.

3. It shot off the end of the ruler.

4. The last ball had all of the energy that was transferred from the prior balls.

14. TESTING DETERGENTS FOR EFFECTIVENESS ON GREASE

1. Answers will vary.

2. Answers will vary.

3. Answers will vary.

4. Because the detergent contains emulsifiers that allow water and oil to mix, making it possible for grease to be lifted off the surface of the item being washed.

15. CREATING AND OBSERVING ANTI-BUBBLES

1. Bubbles are air surrounded by a thin coat of liquid, while anti-bubbles form in liquid with a thin film of air surrounding the fluid.

2. By adding the food coloring, it is easier to see the anti-bubbles.

3. They burst open from the static electricity. The static electricity causes the water in the anti-bubble to become charged, attracting the water below it, bursting it open.

16. USING STEAM TO POWER A BOAT

1. The boat moved.

2. To allow a place from which the heat could escape.

3. This sped up the heating of the water since it did not have to be heated from a completely cold temperature.

4. A rocket works on a similar principle: Every action has an equal and opposite reaction. If a force is created, it will push the object.

17. DETECTING INFRARED RADIATION

1. Answers will vary.

2. Answers will vary.

3. Answers will vary but should be just beyond the red portion of the spectrum. This proves the existence of light rays beyond the visible portion of the spectrum, just beyond red, known as infrared.

18. DETERMINING WHAT COLOR OF LIGHT SHINES BRIGHTEST THROUGH FOG

1. Answers will vary but is most likely the yellow or red light.

2. Answers will vary but is most likely the blue light.

3. The milk was added to make the liquid cloudy, simulating fog.

4. Answers will vary but may include that cars should be equipped with fog lights that emit a certain color of light. Safety lights on the road should emit a certain color that can be most easily seen in fog.

19. MODELING A NUCLEAR REACTION

1. The fission of U-235 splits off 2 neutrons, which in turn strike 2 U-235 atoms, from which 2 neutrons are split, which then strike more U-235 atoms, and so on.

2. With the ruler in the way, not all of the dominoes fell over.

3. The ruler represents the control rod.

20. CREATING A HOLOGRAM

1. Answers will vary but should be yes.

2. It appeared to be above the glass.

3. They are usually made with lasers.

4. Answers will vary.

Tips for Teachers

General

- Always review all safety guidelines before attempting any experiment.
- Enforce all safety guidelines.
- Try the experiment on your own first to be better prepared for possible questions that may arise.
- You may try demonstrating each step of the experiment as you explain it to the students.
- Check for correlation to standards in order to best match the experiment to the curriculum.
- Provide adult assistance and supervision. Do not leave students unsupervised.
- Make sure students feel comfortable asking for help when needed.

Equipment and Supplies

- Most glassware can be purchased from scientific supply companies like Carolina Science Supply Company. Many companies have both print and online catalogs.
- Chemicals and special materials can also be purchased from these companies.
- Many of the supplies and substances used in the experiments are household items that can be found at home or purchased at a local market.
- For some of the hard-to-find items (e.g., extra-large jars), try asking local restaurants, or check warehouse-type stores that carry industrial-size items. For some substances (e.g., lamp oil), you should check with hardware or home-improvement stores.

Special-Needs Students

- Please make sure to follow the individualized education plans (IEPs) and 504 accommodation plans for any special-needs students.
- Provide a handout for students who require visual aids.
- Create a graphic representation of the experiment for students who use picture cards to communicate.

(continued)

- For visually disabled students, provide copies with enlarged print.
- Involve students with dexterity issues by providing opportunities to participate in ways that match their abilities—e.g., be the timekeeper or the instruction reader.
- Read aloud directions for students who require verbal cues.
- Record the instructions for playback.
- Repeat instructions more than once.
- Demonstrate the experiment so that students can see how it is done correctly.
- Check frequently for comprehension.
- Ask students to repeat the information so that you can ensure accuracy.
- Break down directions into simple steps.
- Have students work with a lab partner or in a lab group.
- Provide adult assistance when necessary.
- Make sure that students with auditory disabilities know visual cues in case of danger or emergency.
- Simplify the experiment for students with developmental disabilities.
- Incorporate assistive technology for students who require it; e.g., use of Alphasmart® keyboards for recording observations and for dictation software.
- Provide preferred seating (e.g., front row) for students with disabilities to ensure they are able to see and hear demonstrations.
- Provide an interpreter if available for students with auditory disabilities who require American Sign Language.
- Consult with your school's inclusion specialist, resource teacher, or special education teacher for additional suggestions.
- Arrange furniture so that all students have clear access to information being presented and can move about the room (e.g., wheelchair-accessible aisles of about 48 inches).
- Offer students the option of recording their responses.
- Eliminate background noise when it is distracting.
- Face the class when speaking, and keep your face visible for students who lip-read.
- Repeat new words in various contexts to enhance vocabulary.
- Alter table heights for wheelchair access.
- Substitute equipment with larger sizes for easy gripping.

(continued)

- Ask the student if he or she needs help before offering it.
- Place materials within easy reach of the students.
- Be aware of temperature. Some students may not be able to feel heat or cold and might injure themselves.
- Identify yourself to students with visual impairments. Also speak when you enter or leave the room.
- For visually impaired students, give directions in relation to the student's body. Do not use words like "over here." Also describe verbally what is happening in the experiment.

Glossary

A

acid   a compound capable of neutralizing alkalis and reddening blue litmus paper; containing hydrogen that can be replaced by a metal or an electropositive group to form a salt, or containing an atom that can accept a pair of electros from a base

agate   a type of mineral with curved, colored bands

aggregates   formed by the conjunction or collection of particulars into a mass or sum

amethyst   purple or violet quartz

anti-bubbles   opposite of bubbles; liquid with a thin layer of air surrounding it

astronomer   scientific observer of celestial bodies

atoms   smallest component of an element having the chemical properties of an element

B

barrier   any bar or obstacle that obstructs progress or access

base   fundamental principle or ground work, or bottom support

Bernoulli's principle   the pressure in a stream of fluid or air is reduced as the speed of flow is increased

black light   invisible infrared or ultraviolet light

bonds   things that bind, fasten, confine, or hold together

boron   non-metallic element occurring naturally only in combination and obtained in either an amorphous or a crystalline form when reduced from its compounds

boundary layer   the portion of a fluid past a body that is in the immediate vicinity of the body and that has a reduced flow due to the forces of adhesion and viscosity

C

cadmium   white, ductile, divalent metallic element resembling tin, used in plating and in making certain alloys

calcium carbonate   white, crystalline, water-insoluble, tasteless powder occurring in nature in various forms as calcite, chalk, and limestone

calcium sulfate   white calcium salt used especially as a diluent in tablets and in hydrated form as plaster of paris

carbon dioxide   colorless, odorless, incombustible gas present in the atmosphere and formed during respiration

cement   any of various calcined mixtures of clay and limestone, usually mixed with water, sand, or gravel to form concrete used as a building material

chain reaction   reaction that results in a product necessary for the continuance of the reaction

chemical   substance produced by or used in a chemical process

chemical energy   liberated by a chemical reaction or absorbed in the formation of a chemical compound

chemical reaction   process that involves changes in the structure and energy content of atoms, molecules, or ions

citric acid   tribasic acid having a strong acidic taste; an intermediate in the metabolism of carbohydrates occurring in many fruits such as limes and lemons; obtained chiefly by fermentation of crude sugar or corn sugar

clockwise   in the direction of the rotation of the hands of a clock as viewed from the front

clotting   a semi-solid mass such as coagulated blood

coagulate   to change from a fluid into a thickened mass; coagulation

combustion   rapid oxidation accompanied by heat and light

complex   composed of many interconnected parts

concentration   exclusive attention to one object

consistency   a degree of density, firmness, and viscosity

control rod   neutron-absorbing material, such as boron or cadmium, in the shape of a rod or other configuration, that can be moved into or out of the core of a nuclear reactor to regulate the rate of fission

counterclockwise   in the direction opposite to the rotation of the hands of a clock as viewed from the front

crystal   clear, transparent mineral or glass resembling ice

crystallize   to form into crystals

culinary   pertaining to or used in cooking or the kitchen

D

denature   to change the structure of a substance so that it loses its original properties

diffusers   items that hold a substance at a high concentration and allow the substance to diffuse to the surroundings at a lower concentration

diffusion	passive movement of particles from an area of higher concentration to an area of lower concentration
digestion	process by which food is broken up physically, as by the action of the teeth, and chemically or with the help of enzymes, and converted into a substance suitable for absorption into the body
digestive system	the system by which ingested food is acted upon by physical and chemical means to provide the body with absorbable nutrients
discomfort	absence of comfort or ease
dissolution rate	the time taken for a solute to dissolve in a solvent
dissolve	to cause the particles of a solute to become suspended in a solvent

E

electrical energy	energy made available by the flow of an electric charge through a conductor
electromagnetic spectrum	the entire spectrum considered as a continuum of electric, magnetic, and visible radiation
electron	negatively charged sub-atomic particle
elements	a class of substances that cannot be separated into simpler substances by chemical means
emigrate	to leave one region to settle into another
emulsifier	substance that helps an emulsion form or helps keep an emulsion from separating
endothermic	chemical change that is accompanied by absorption of heat
energy	capacity to do work
enzymes	any of various proteins originating from living cells capable of producing certain chemical changes in organic substances by catalytic action, as in digestion
equilibrium	state of rest or balance due to the equal action of opposing forces
evaporate	to change from a liquid state into vapor
exothermic	a chemical change that is accompanied by a liberation of heat

F

fatty acid	any of the monocarboxylic acids that form part of a lipid molecule and can be derived from fat by hydrolysis
fluid	liquid or gas that changes in shape and form
fluoresce	emission of electromagnetic radiation light by a substance that has absorbed radiation of a different wavelength

fog   droplets of water vapor suspended in the air near the ground

force   a powerful effect or influence caused through pressure

fragrance   distinctive odor or aroma

frequency   number of occurrences within a given time period

friction   force resisting the relative lateral motion of solid surfaces

G

gas   state of matter distinguished from the solid and liquid states by relatively low density and viscosity and relatively great expansion and contraction with changes in pressure and temperature

geode   hollow rock or nodule, with its cavity usually lined with crystals

geological science   deals with the history of the Earth as recorded in rocks

gravity   force of attraction between all masses in the universe

groundwater   water located beneath the ground in pore spaces of soil and in the fractures of lithologic formations

gypsum   common white or colorless mineral used to make cement and plaster

H

hologram   the intermediate photograph that contains information for reproducing a 3-dimensional image by holography

holographic image   a hologram

hydraulic cements   cement materials that require water

hydrocarbon   organic compound containing only carbon and hydrogen

hydrogen   non-metallic, univalent element that is normally a colorless and odorless highly flammable diatomic gas

I

inadvertently   without knowledge or intention

infrared radiation   electromagnetic radiation with wavelengths longer than visible light but shorter than radio waves

insoluble   incapable of being dissolved

integral   existing as an essential constituent or characteristic

intensity   amount of energy transmitted

ion   particle that is electrically charged, such as an atom or molecule that has lost or gained one or more electrons

ionic   containing or involving in the forms of ions

K

kinetic energy   the mechanical energy that a body has by virtue of its motion

L

lactase   an enzyme capable of hydrolyzing lactose into glucose and galactose

lactose intolerance   inability to hydrolyze lactose, thus the inability to digest milk products

laser   device that produces a nearly parallel, monochromatic, and coherent beam of light by exciting atoms to a higher energy level and causing them to radiate their energy in phase; an acronym for "light amplification by simulated emission of radiation"

lava   molten, fluid rock that issues from a volcano or volcanic vent

light meter   exposure meter

limestone   sedimentary rock consisting predominantly of calcium carbonate and often used as building stone

linear accelerator   accelerator in which particles are propelled in straight paths by the use of alternating electric voltages timed in such a way that the particles receive increasing increments of energy

liquid   substance composed of molecules that move freely among themselves but do not tend to separate like those of gases

longitude   the angular distance on the Earth or on a map, east or west of the prime meridian, to the point of the Earth's surface for which the longitude is being ascertained; expressed in degrees, hours, minutes, or seconds

longitudinal   placed or running lengthwise

M

matter   substance or substances of which any physical object is composed

mechanical energy   the combination of potential and kinetic energy of a machine or machine part

membrane   thin, pliable sheet or layer

meteorology   the science dealing with the atmosphere and its phenomena, including weather and climate

microwave   an electromagnetic wave of extremely high frequency

minerals   any of a class of substances occurring in nature

mixture   any combination or blend of different elements

molecules   the smallest physical unit of an element or compound

N

nuclear fission   splitting the nucleus of an atom into nuclei of lighter atoms, accompanied by the release of energy

nuclear reactor   large container for processes in which the substances involved undergo a chemical reaction

O

obscures   clouds or hides

optics   the branch of physical science that deals with vision and with the properties and phenomena of both visible and invisible light

P

paddle wheel   a waterwheel made of scoops set around a wheel

photographic   pertaining to photographs

photographic plate a flat sheet of metal or glass on which a photographic image can be recorded

plaster of paris   hydrated form of calcium sulfate

potential energy   stored energy

precipitate   a solid substance formed as a result of a chemical reaction

propel   to push forward with a force

properties   characteristics

propulsion   a propelling force

protein   large molecule composed of one ore more amino acids

Q

quartz   one of the most common minerals with many varieties that differ in color, luster, and other characteristics; it is piezoelectric and used to control the frequencies of radio transmitters

R

radiant energy   energy transmitted by electromagnetic waves

radiation   the process in which energy is emitted as particles or waves

radiation therapy   treatment of disease by means of X-ray or radioactive substances

S

salt	any class of compounds formed by the replacement of one or more hydrogen atoms of an acid with elements or groups composed of anions and cations that usually ionize in solution
sediment	mineral or organic matter deposited by water, air, or ice
sedimentary	formed by the deposition of sediment in reference to rocks
semi-solid	having a somewhat firm consistency
sodium	soft, silver-white, metallic element that oxidizes rapidly in moist air
solid	having relative firmness; coherence of particles as matter that is not liquid or gaseous
state	the condition of matter with respect to structure, form, and phase
steamboat	a steam-driven vessel
substance	that of which a thing consists of in its physical matter; material
supernate	the fluid above the precipitate
supersaturated	to increase the concentration of a solution beyond saturation

T

telescope	instrument designed for the observation of remote objects by the collection of electromagnetic radiation
texture	the feel of a surface or a fabric
thermal energy	energy in the form of heat
three-dimensional	having depth as well as height and width (or the illusion of)
trajectory	the path followed by an object moving through space
transverse	situated or lying across
turbine	a rotary engine that extracts energy from a fluid or airflow and converts it into useful work
two-dimensional	a figure that has length and width but no depth

U

ultraviolet	radiation lying in the range beyond violet that has wavelengths shorter than light but longer than X-rays
uranium-235	uranium isotope with mass number 235, capable of sustaining chain reactions

V

velocity	rapidity of motion or operation

visible-light spectrum   the portion of the electromagnetic spectrum visible to the human eye

volcanic   igneous rock produced by eruption and solidified on or near the Earth's surface

W

water soluble   capable of dissolving in water

water vapor   a dispersion in air of molecules of water produced by evaporation

wavelength   the distance measured in the direction of propagation of a wave between two successive points in the wave that are characterized by the same phase of oscillation

waves   progressive disturbances propagated from point to point as in transmission of sound or light

Appendix of Useful Charts and Diagrams

This appendix has been provided as a general resource for physical science experiments and education. The following charts and diagrams are helpful not just for the experiments contained in this volume but also for use with other physical-science–related activities in present or future studies.

The first chart contains information regarding the metric system, also known as the International System of Units (abbreviated SI from the French *Le Système International d'Unités*), which is the standard of measurement in scientific experimentation. When experiments are performed and documented in scientific studies, all units are in SI. However, in the United States, students are still educated using English units, so a second chart with conversions to the metric system of measurement has also been provided.

Note also a figure demonstrating the colors of the pH scale. In many chemistry experiments, the pH of a substance is crucial in the observation of a reaction. Thus, the color chart is essential for properly identifying where on the pH scale a substance is categorized. Examples of materials that typically have a designated pH are provided to help the experimenter make sense of his or her observations.

Additionally, Newton's three Laws of Motion are described in both text and figures. These, we trust, allow the student to visualize the Laws of Motion and apply them to the experiments in this volume as well as to future studies of physics. Next, simple machines—on which complex machines are based—are illustrated.

Finally, the all-important Periodic Table of the Elements has been included. The table can be used as a reference for experiments in this volume as well as for the study of chemistry. Atomic numbers, atomic symbols, and atomic weights are included in the chart.

It is our hope that these additional resources will serve as a reference for students and educators in the field of science, not only for the topics covered in this volume but also for future courses or activities in chemistry and physics.

Metric Prefix Chart

Common Metric Prefixes	Unit Multiples
kilo	1,000
hecto	100
deca	10
deci	0.1
centi	0.01
milli	0.001

Base units: **length**: meter; **volume**: liter; **mass**: gram.

U.S. Measurements to Metric Conversions

Length

1 centimeter (cm)	= 10 millimeters (mm)
1 inch (in)	= 2.54 centimeters
1 foot (ft)	= 0.3048 meters (m)
1 foot	= 12 inches
1 yard	= 3 feet
1 meter	= 100 centimeters
1 meter	= 3.280839895 feet
1 furlong	= 660 feet
1 kilometer (km)	= 1,000 meters
1 kilometer	= 0.62137119 miles
1 mile	= 5280 feet
1 mile	= 1.609344 kilometers
1 nautical mile	= 1.852 kilometers

Area

1 square foot	= 144 square inches
1 square foot	= 929.0304 square centimeters
1 square yard	= 9 square feet
1 square meter	= 10.7639104 square feet
1 acre	= 43,560 square feet
1 hectare	= 10,000 square meters
1 hectare	= 2.4710538 acres
1 square kilometer	= 100 hectares
1 square mile	= 2.58998811 square kilometers
1 square mile	= 640 acres

Speed

1 mile per hour (mph)	= 1.46666667 feet per second (fps)
1 mile per hour (mph)	= 1.609344 kilometers per hour (kph)
1 knot	= 1.150779448 miles per hour (mph)
1 foot per second	= 0.68181818 miles per hour
1 kilometer per hour	= 0.62137119 miles per hour

Volume

1 US tablespoon (tbsp)	= 3 US teaspoons (tsp)
1 US fluid ounce (fl oz)	= 29.57353 milliliters (ml)
1 US cup	= 16 US tablespoons
1 US cup	= 8 US fluid ounces
1 US pint	= 2 US cups
1 US pint	= 16 US fluid ounces
1 liter (L)	= 33.8140227 US fluid ounces
1 liter	= 1,000 milliliters
1 US quart	= 2 US pints
1 US gallon	= 4 US quarts
1 US gallon	= 3.78541178 liters

Weight

1 milligram (mg)	= 0.001 grams (g)

1 gram	= 0.001 kilograms (kg)
1 gram	= 0.035273962 ounces (oz)
1 ounce	= 28.34952312 grams
1 ounce	= 0.0625 pounds (lb)
1 pound	= 16 ounces
1 pound	= 0.45359237 kilograms
1 kilogram	= 1,000 grams
1 kilogram	= 35.273962 ounces
1 kilogram	= 2.20462262 pounds
1 stone	= 14 pounds
1 short ton	= 2,000 pounds
1 metric ton	= 1,000 kilograms

Temperature

Degrees Celsius

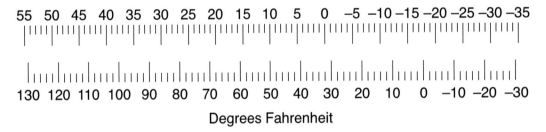

Degrees Fahrenheit

Taken from: http://www.metricconversioncharts.org/

pH Scale

Concentration of hydrogen ions compared to distilled water		Examples of solutions at this pH
10,000,000	pH = 0	Battery acid, strong hydrofluoric acid
1,000,000	pH = 1	Hydrochloric acid secreted by stomach lining
100,000	pH = 2	Lemon juice, gastric acid, vinegar
10,000	pH = 3	Grapefruit, orange juice, soda
1,000	pH = 4	Acid rain, tomato juice
100	pH = 5	Soft drinking water, black coffee
10	pH = 6	Urine, saliva
1	pH = 7	"Pure" water
1/10	pH = 8	Sea water
1/1,00	pH = 9	Baking soda
1/1,000	pH = 10	Great Salt Lake, milk of magnesia
1/10,000	pH = 11	Ammonia solution
1/100,000	pH = 12	Soapy water
1/1,000,000	pH = 13	Beaches, oven cleaner
1/10,000,000	pH = 14	Liquid drain cleaner

EBNER Physical Science Experiments Figure App 5

Newton's Laws of Motion

First Law of Motion

An object at rest will remain at rest unless acted on by an unbalanced force. An object in motion continues in motion with the same speed and in the same direction unless acted upon by an unbalanced force. This law is often called "the law of inertia."

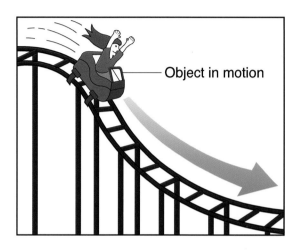

Object in motion

Second Law of Motion

Acceleration is produced when a force (F) acts on a mass (m). The greater the mass of the object being accelerated, the greater the amount of force needed to accelerate the object (v = velocity).

Force

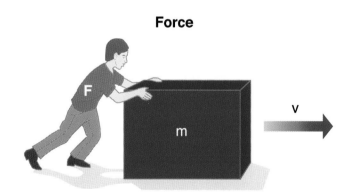

Third Law of Motion

For every action there is an equal and opposite reaction.

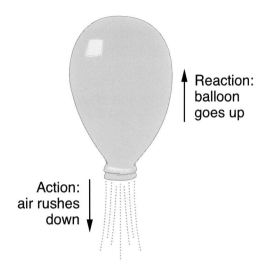

Reaction: balloon goes up

Action: air rushes down

Information quoted from: http://teachertech.rice.edu/Participants/louviere/Newton/

Simple Machines

Identify these simple "machines" and discover how they are used.

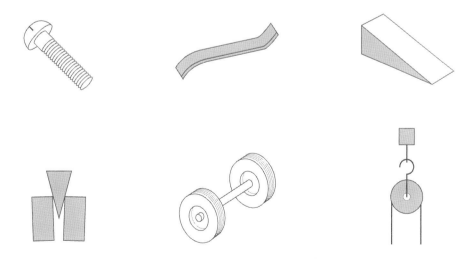

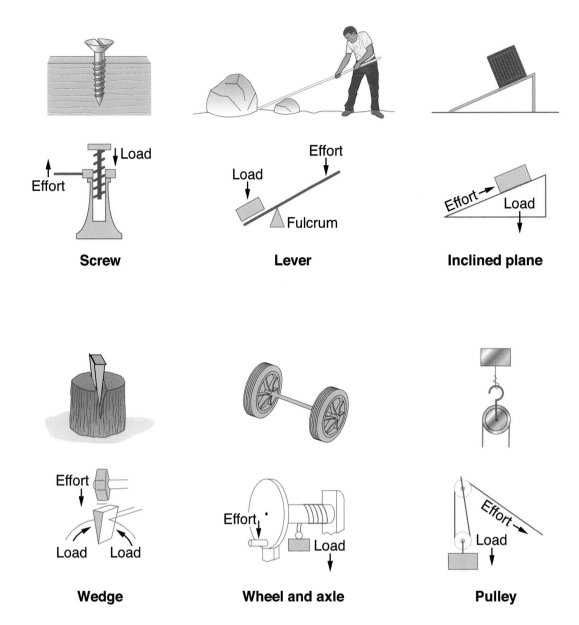

Screw

Lever

Inclined plane

Wedge

Wheel and axle

Pulley

Periodic Table of Elements

Periodic Table of Elements

Legend:
- 1 — atomic number
- H — symbol
- 1.008 — atomic weight

Numbers in parentheses are the atomic mass numbers of radioactive isotopes.

1	2	3	4	5	6	7	8	9	10	11	12	13	14	15	16	17	18
1 H 1.008																	2 He 4.003
3 Li 6.941	4 Be 9.012											5 B 10.81	6 C 12.01	7 N 14.01	8 O 16.00	9 F 19.00	10 Ne 20.18
11 Na 22.99	12 Mg 24.31											13 Al 26.98	14 Si 28.09	15 P 30.97	16 S 32.07	17 Cl 35.45	18 Ar 39.95
19 K 39.10	20 Ca 40.08	21 Sc 44.96	22 Ti 47.88	23 V 50.94	24 Cr 52.00	25 Mn 54.94	26 Fe 55.85	27 Co 58.93	28 Ni 58.69	29 Cu 63.55	30 Zn 65.39	31 Ga 69.72	32 Ge 72.59	33 As 74.92	34 Se 78.96	35 Br 79.90	36 Kr 83.80
37 Rb 85.47	38 Sr 87.62	39 Y 88.91	40 Zr 91.22	41 Nb 92.91	42 Mo 95.94	43 Tc (98)	44 Ru 101.1	45 Rh 102.9	46 Pd 106.4	47 Ag 107.9	48 Cd 112.4	49 In 114.8	50 Sn 118.7	51 Sb 121.8	52 Te 127.6	53 I 126.9	54 Xe 131.3
55 Cs 132.9	56 Ba 137.3	57-71*	72 Hf 178.5	73 Ta 180.9	74 W 183.9	75 Re 186.2	76 Os 190.2	77 Ir 192.2	78 Pt 195.1	79 Au 197.0	80 Hg 200.6	81 Tl 204.4	82 Pb 207.2	83 Bi 209.0	84 Po (210)	85 At (210)	86 Rn (222)
87 Fr (223)	88 Ra (226)	89-103‡	104 Rf (261)	105 Db (262)	106 Sg (263)	107 Bh (262)	108 Hs (265)	109 Mt (266)	110 Ds (271)	111 Rg (272)	112 Uub (285)	113 Uut (284)	114 Uuq (289)	115 Uup (288)	116 Uuh		118 Uuo

*lanthanide series

57 La 138.9	58 Ce 140.1	59 Pr 140.9	60 Nd 144.2	61 Pm (145)	62 Sm 150.4	63 Eu 152.0	64 Gd 157.3	65 Tb 158.9	66 Dy 162.5	67 Ho 164.9	68 Er 167.3	69 Tm 168.9	70 Yb 173.0	71 Lu 175.0

‡actinide series

89 Ac (227)	90 Th 232.0	91 Pa 231.0	92 U 238.0	93 Np (237)	94 Pu (244)	95 Am (243)	96 Cm (247)	97 Bk (247)	98 Cf (251)	99 Es (252)	100 Fm (257)	101 Md (258)	102 No (259)	103 Lr (260)

Internet Resources

The Internet is a wealth of information and resources for students, parents, and teachers. However, all sources should be verified for fact, and it is recommended never to rely on any single source for in-depth research. The following list of resources is a sample of what the World Wide Web has to offer. The sites listed were accessible as of January 3, 2011.

American Library Association. Available online. URL: http://www.ala.org/gwstemplate.cfm?section=greatwebsites&template=/cfapps/gws/displaysection.cfm&sec=29. Accessed January 3, 2011. Links to Web sites about chemistry and physics recommended by the American Library Association are provided, along with recommendations by age level.

Ask the Van. "Why Does a Black Light Make Objects Glow?" Available online. URL: http://van.physics.illinois.edu/qa/listing.php?id=1913. Accessed January 3, 2011. Web site from the University of Illinois physics department that succinctly explains how a black light works.

Association of Lifecasters International. "A brief History of Plaster and Gypsum." Available online. URL: http://www.artmolds.com/ali/history_plaster.html. Accessed January 3, 2011. Starting with ancient times, this article discusses the development and use of plaster.

Desertusa.com. "Geodes." Available online. URL: http://www.desertusa.com/magjan98/jan_pap/du_rock_geode.html. Accessed January 3, 2011. Explains how geodes are made and where to find them.

Discovery Education. Available online. URL:http://www.discoveryschool.com. Accessed January 3, 2011. Informational site that contains lessons and links for educational purposes.

eHow. Available online. URL: http://www.ehow.com/. Accessed January 3, 2011. Web site that has links to videos on how to do various activities, including science activities.

Energy Quest. Available online. URL: http://www.energyquest.ca.gov/. Accessed January 3, 2011. Web site that has sections for students and educators regarding energy sources and uses, created by the California Energy Commission.

Exploratorium. Available online. URL: http://www.exploratorium.edu. Accessed January 3, 2011. Web site with numerous chemistry and physical science related activities and experiments, along with lesson plans for teachers.

Georgia State University. "Diffusion." Available online. URL: http://hyperphysics.phy-astr.gsu.edu/hbase/kinetic/diffus.html. Accessed January 3, 2011. Explanations and diagrams of diffusion and diffusion rates as presented by a member of the physics department of Georgia State University.

———. "Magnetic Fields." Available online. URL: http://hyperphysics.phy-astr.gsu.edu/hbase/magnetic/magfie.html. Accessed January 3, 2011. Explanations and diagrams of how magnetic fields work.

———. "Nuclear Reactions." Available online. URL: http://hyperphysics.phy-astr.gsu.edu/hbase/nuclear/nucrea.html. Accessed January 3, 2011. Explanations, definitions, diagrams, and links related to nuclear reactions.

———. "Visible Light." Available online. URL: http://hyperphysics.phy-astr.gsu.edu/hbase/ems3.html. Accessed January 3, 2011. Explanation of the visible light spectrum, along with diagrams and links.

How Stuff Works. "How Black Lights Work." Available online. URL: http://science.howstuffworks.com/innovation/black-light.htm. Accessed January 3, 2011. Explains in simple terms how a black light works and the visual effect on white items. Includes links to video demonstrations.

Koehler, Kenneth. "Nuclear Reactions" Available online. URL: http://www.rwc.uc.edu/koehler/biophys/7b.html. Accessed January 3, 2011. Explains different types of nuclear reactions.

Littleshop.physics.colostate.edu. "Bernoulli's Principle." Available online. URL: http://littleshop.physics.colostate.edu/Videos/Pressure/bernoulli/bernoulli.html. Accessed January 3, 2011. Web site from Colorado State University with a video demonstrating and explaining Bernoulli's Principle.

Massachusetts Institute of Technology. "Holography: The Light Fantastic." Available online. URL: http://web.mit.edu/museum/exhibitions/holography.html. Accessed January 3, 2011. Information about a hologram display at the MIT museum.

Mayo Clinic. "Lactose Intolerance." Available online. URL: http://www.mayoclinic.com/health/lactose-intolerance/DS00530. Accessed January 3, 2011. Information from the Mayo Clinic regarding symptoms and treatment of lactose intolerance.

Medicinenet.com. "Lactose Intolerance." Available online. URL: http://www.medicinenet.com/lactose_intolerance/article.htm. Accessed January 3, 2011. General information about the symptoms, causes, and treatment of lactose intolerance.

Memorial University of Newfoundland. "Principles of Diffusion and Osmosis." Available online. URL: http://www.mun.ca/biology/Osmosis_Diffusion/tutor2.html. Accessed January 3, 2011. Web site with tutorials, interaction questions, and answers, along with information on diffusion.

Mitchell, Mark. "Animated Demonstration of Bernoulli's Principle." Available online. URL: http://home.earthlink.net/~mmc1919/venturi.html. Accessed January 3, 2011. An article with animations demonstrating Bernoulli's Principle, explanations of how it relates to curve balls, and links to related information.

National Digestive Diseases Information Clearinghouse. "Lactose Intolerance." Available online. URL: http://digestive.niddk.nih.gov/ddiseases/pubs/lactoseintolerance/. Accessed January 3, 2011. Defines lactose intolerance, explains the symptoms, and offers forms of treatment.

Newirth, Terry. "Properties of Water." Available online. URL: http://www.haverford.edu/educ/knight-booklet/propofwater.htm. Accessed January 3, 2011. Explanation of the properties of water and how different properties impact the interaction of water, salts, detergents, and oils.

Physics-edu.org. "Understanding Chemical Reactions." Available online. URL: http://physics-edu.org/chemical_reaction.htm. Accessed January 3, 2011. Explains chemical reactions, including both endothermic and exothermic reactions.

Reusch, William. "Polymers." Available online. URL: http://www2.chemistry.msu.edu/faculty/reusch/VirtTxtJml/polymers.htm. Accessed January 3, 2011. Detailed explanation of the formation of polymers along with their structures.

Rocksforkids.com. "Geodes." Available online. URL: http://www.rocksforkids.com/R&M/geodes.html. Accessed January 3, 2011. Web site with color photographs of geodes.

Rocks4u.com. "Rock Hounding Essential Information: Dugway, Utah, Geode Beds." Available online. URL: http://www.rocks4u.com/geodebed.htm. Accessed January 3, 2011. Web site with specific information on and maps for finding geodes.

South Caroline Department of Natural Resources. "What Is Photosynthesis?" Available online. URL: http://www.dnr.sc.gov/ael/personals/pjpb/lecture/lecture.html. Accessed January 3, 2011. Article includes diagram of the visible light spectrum.

United States Armed Forces. "A History of Steamboats." Available online. URL: http://montgomery.sam.usace.army.mil/educational/5thand6th/ahistoryofsteamboats.pdf. Accessed January 3, 2011. Pamphlet from the U.S. Army that reviews the history of the steamboat.

Universe Today. "Infrared Light." Available online. URL: http://www.universetoday.com/34504/infrared-light/. Accessed January 3, 2011. Defines and presents applications for the use of infrared light.

Index